PROFESSOR SWEET has made a careful study of the development of the Church in America as an expression of the religious motive of the people. He tells of the beginning of the Church in the colonies and traces the signs and fruitage of religious interest in the establishment of the various churches in the ever-expanding nation. The story of each of the more prominent denominations is recited. There is an illuminating chapter on Church government and one on Church federation and union. The volume is rich in reliable information relative to the history of Church organization and life in America.

STUDIES IN CHRISTIAN FAITH

Henry H. Meyer, Editor

Wade Crawford Barclay, Associate Editor

OUR AMERICAN CHURCHES

By

WILLIAM W. SWEET

Approved by the Committee on Curriculum
of the Board of Sunday Schools of the
Methodist Episcopal Church

THE METHODIST BOOK CONCERN

NEW YORK   CINCINNATI

To
THE MEMBERS OF MY SEMINAR
AT DEPAUW UNIVERSITY,
1923–24

CONTENTS

INTRODUCTION

THE conviction deepens in the minds of many that closer cooperation among the various denominational bodies in the United States is a first essential to either thorough or rapid progress toward the realization of the kingdom of God. There can be no genuine cooperation without mutual respect based upon understanding. Each denomination, with its peculiar denominational emphases in matters of rite, ceremonies, polity, and creed, has a historical background that must be known if the genius of the denomination is to be understood. Prejudice, lack of respect, and intolerance all are due in no slight degree to lack of information. One cannot know the life story of any one of our American churches without being conscious of a heightened appreciation. Consecration, devotion, sacrificial labors enter in abundant measure into the story of each. Wide as may be the differences among the denominations, certain inheritances they have in common, and an acquaintance with these, forms a certain basis of understanding and a preparation for cooperation. *Our American Churches,* it is believed, will go far toward giving this acquaintance. The writer has been for years a thorough student of church history and has given special attention to the history of the churches of the United States.

A growing demand is expressed for elective courses for young people's classes. The series "Studies in Christian Faith" has been produced and is offered in response to this demand. Two titles in the series—*Christianity for To-day: a Brief Study of the Christian Faith,* by Professor John G. Hill, of the University of Southern California; and *Our American Churches,* by Professor William W. Sweet, of DePauw University—are published simultaneously, and other titles will soon appear.

THE EDITORS.

CHAPTER I

THE RELIGIOUS MOTIVE IN AMERICAN COLONIZATION

IT is interesting and significant to remember that just twenty-five years after Columbus made his famous voyage of discovery in 1492, Martin Luther nailed his ninety-five theses to the door of the church at Wittenberg (1517). This act marks the opening of the Protestant Reformation. Thus, the discovery of America and the beginning of Protestantism are contemporary events. As time passed, these two great historic events came to be more and more closely connected in their historical significance.

If we are to understand the various American churches of to-day, it will be necessary for us to take a brief glance, at least, at conditions in England and in Western Europe, especially during the seventeenth century.

The great English colonizing period.—England was slow in founding colonies in America. She was over a century behind Spain in this respect and nearly a century behind Portugal. The first Spanish colony—Isabella, on the island of Haiti—was founded by Columbus on his second expedition in 1493. The Portuguese established their first American settlement in South America as early as 1530. Indeed, it was not until England became a Protestant nation that motives were created which led to the English colonization of America. After England became definitely Protestant, toward the close of the sixteenth century, in the reign of Queen Elizabeth, English voyagers and colonizers became extremely active, and the great English colonies in America, and, indeed, we might say with equal truth, the great British Empire were the result.

English motives in colonization.—There have been numerous motives in colonization. Perhaps the primitive and original motive is trade. This was the motive back of the colonization of the ancient Greeks and Phœnicians, which led to the establishment of the Phœnician colony at Carthage and the Greek colonies in southern Italy. It was one of the English motives also; for just about the time America was discovered, England was beginning to manufacture more goods than she could consume, and her merchants were seeking new markets. Then there was the patriotic motive—the desire to extend English dominion. When Spain became the arch enemy of England, in the latter part of Queen Elizabeth's reign, Englishmen conceived the idea that one way to combat Spain was to found rival colonies. This was always a strong motive in the mind of Sir Walter Raleigh; for no Englishman was more inveterate in his hatred of Spain than he, and his two attempts at founding colonies in America were largely the outgrowth of this motive. Still another motive was romance and adventure, and England in the sixteenth and seventeenth centuries had many romantic adventurers. Francis Drake and John Hawkins are examples of this type of Englishman, and their daring deeds and bold adventures, though accompanied by injustice and cruelty, were important contributions to English colonization. *The most important single motive in English colonization, however, was the religious motive.* To comprehend this motive it is necessary to understand the nature of the Protestant Reformation in England.

The Protestant Reformation in England.—When the Lutheran movement began in Germany it met a hearty response in England. The way had been prepared a century before by the morning star of the Reformation— John Wycliffe. As a result the writings of Martin Luther found many readers in England. Luther's teachings likewise found a place in the great English universities— Oxford and Cambridge. At Cambridge a group met regularly to discuss Luther's writings. Because of that fact they were called "the Germans." At first Henry VIII, the king of England, was violently opposed to Luther and the reformers and even wrote a pamphlet against them, for which he received from the Pope the title "Defender of the Faith," a title the English kings still use. The Reformation in England naturally falls into four divisions: (1) the break with Rome, which occurred in the reign of Henry VIII; (2) the transformation of the English Church into a Protestant Church during the reign of Edward VI; (3) the Catholic reaction under Mary Tudor, or "Bloody Mary"; and (4) the completion of the Reformation under Queen Elizabeth.

King Henry VIII.—As is well known, the separation of the English Church from the Roman Catholic Church was brought about through the desire of Henry VIII to obtain a divorce from his Spanish wife, Catherine of Aragon. It will be impossible here to enter into all the motives back of the English king's action in the matter of his divorce. The king had always been troubled about the legitimacy of his marriage, since his marriage with Catherine, his deceased brother's widow, had only been consummated through a special papal dispensation. Like all kings, Henry was eager to have a male heir to succeed him, and the queen's failure to bear him an heir came to be considered by the king as a judgment of God upon the marriage. There was doubtless also a large element of sordidness in the king's desire for the divorce—his lust for the beautiful Anne Boleyn. But, whatever the motives back of the king's action, this much is true: the English nation, especially the great mass of the laity, was undoubtedly willing to have the break take place.

The break with Rome.—The Pope refused, though not for moral reasons, to grant the divorce desired by the English king. The king now saw that the only way to gain his desire was to settle matters in his own courts, and this he proceeded to do. The result was that the English Church was separated from papal control, and the king, by an act of Parliament, was declared supreme head of the Church in England. Thomas Cranmer, who had been one of the "Germans" at Cambridge, was appointed Archbishop of Canterbury; and other men, such as Hugh Latimer, for example, who were known to favor the doctrines of the Reformation, were appointed to other bishoprics. New articles of faith were adopted which attempted to steer a middle course between Lutheranism and Romanism. The Bible was officially translated into English, the official translation—a combination of Tyndale's version and the version of Miles Coverdale—printed by Thomas Matthew and known as Matthew's Bible. The many monasteries, shrines, and relics were destroyed throughout England. This was an unmitigated blessing even though the greedy king did get most of the spoil from their destruction. Although these changes in the church were sweeping, there was little change in doctrine and practice. The English Church under Henry VIII was still largely Roman Catholic in most respects, but no longer recognized the Pope at Rome.

The transformation of the English Church.—When Edward VI, the only son of Henry VIII, came to the throne, he was a mere boy. Before his death Henry had provided that a council of regency should carry on the government. This council, being under the control of the reform party, immediately began to make changes in the church. The church service, formerly conducted in Latin, was now conducted in English. The sermon in this new service was given a much more important place, and a version of the Psalms in meter was made to be sung in public worship. Thus congregational singing was introduced into the English Church. It was also provided that the Lord's Supper should be given in both kinds; that is, both bread and wine should be given to the people. (The Roman Catholic Church had administered only bread to the laity.) In 1549 the first prayer book was published in English. Three years later a second prayer book was issued in which the whole idea of the Catholic mass was done away with, the word "altar" giving place to "table," and "priest" to "minister." This last prayer book is the basis of the present English prayer book, and it is from this book that the Methodist ritual is largely taken. A new statement of doctrine followed, known as the Forty-two Articles, which became the basis for the Thirty-nine Articles of Elizabeth's day, and they in turn the basis for the Twenty-five Methodist Articles.

The Catholic reaction.—Edward VI, the frail boy king, died of consumption after a reign of six years. He was succeeded by the Princess Mary, daughter of the much-wronged Catharine of Aragon, the divorced first wife of Henry VIII. Naturally Mary had been raised a devout

Catholic and came to the throne with a consuming desire to restore England to obedience to Rome. To make things worse for the English Protestants she married the bigoted Philip II of Spain. Immediately the queen began to remove Protestant bishops from their seats, and Catholic bishops were restored. Those who, under Edward VI, had been the most active in making the church Protestant were imprisoned, and four horrible years of persecution began. This persecution stained indelibly the memory of the queen and fastened upon her the name "Bloody Mary." The total number of Queen Mary's victims was about three hundred, "a total greater than that in Henry VIII's reign of thirty-eight years or Elizabeth's of forty-five." The victims included many faithful ministers of flocks and humble tillers of the soil and artisans, besides several bishops and the Archbishop of Canterbury— Thomas Cranmer. In October, 1555, two well-known bishops—Latimer and Ridley—were burned at Oxford. We are told that at the stake Latimer called to his companion: "Be of good comfort, Master Ridley. We shall this day light such a candle by God's grace in England as, I trust, shall never be put out." While in prison Cranmer, the deposed archbishop, had recanted six times; but, finally, when his time came to face death, his courage returned, and, placing his right hand first into the flame, he cried, "This which hath sinned, having signed the writing, must be the first to suffer punishment." The martyrdom of Bishops Ridley and Latimer did indeed light the torch, and that of Cranmer spread the conflagration, which in the end burned up the Roman Catholic reaction and made England a Protestant nation. In numerous other ways Queen Mary attempted to restore Catholicism to England. She tried to rebuild the English monasteries and revive pilgrimages to shrines; but the English people had little enthusiasm for these medieval practices and institutions. Meanwhile the sad and disappointed queen was hastening to her death, and in May, 1558, Mary, "the unhappiest of queens and wives and women," died. The daughter of Anne Boleyn—the Princess Elizabeth—came to the English throne, and with her came a new Act of Supremacy and a new zeal for Protestantism.

The completion of the Reformation.—The coming of Elizabeth to the throne of England meant the permanent triumph of the Protestant party. In 1559 Parliament, after a hard struggle, passed two acts, the first of which, known as the "Act of Supremacy," declared the queen the Supreme Governor of the Church, the second, called the "Act of Uniformity of Common Prayer," attempting to compel the use of a newly revised prayer book and to prohibit all others. Of course, the Catholics refused to recognize Queen Elizabeth as the rightful ruler, and the French and Spanish kings tried every means in their power to drive her from the throne. Catholic plots were numerous. Mary, the beautiful Queen of Scotland, being a Catholic, sought to gain the English throne. In this endeavor she was supported by the French and Spanish rulers. All these Catholic attempts, however, were in vain; for the people of England rallied more and more enthusiastically about their queen, and thus Protestantism and patriotism came to mean one and the same thing in the days of Queen Elizabeth.

The rise of Protestant extremists.—During the reign of "Bloody Mary" many English Protestants had fled to the Continent to escape persecution, and there they came in contact with a type of extreme Protestants, especially in Switzerland and southern Germany. When Elizabeth came to the throne, these exiles returned to England, bringing with them their more extreme Protestant notions. While this was going on in England, Presbyterianism was gaining a foothold in Scotland. The Scotch rulers tried to uphold Catholicism, but a strong Protestant party, aided by the nobles, finally succeeded in overthrowing the Catholic party. By the year 1558 Protestantism had gained the ascendancy in Scotland. The great leader of this Protestant movement in Scotland was John Knox, who, as an exile in Geneva, Switzerland, had come to accept Calvin's system of doctrine and church government.

The beginning of divisions.—It was not long until there appeared at least three groups among the more extreme Protestants in England, to all of whom we might apply the term "Puritans." These various Puritan groups were: first, the moderates, who wished to remain in the Church of England, but who desired to purify its services from the forms and ceremonies that savored of Rome; secondly, the Presbyterians, who desired completely to change the form of church government and substitute the Presbyterian form for the Episcopal, or rule by bishops; thirdly, the separatists, who later were known as Independents, or Congregationalists, and who insisted on the right of each congregation to manage its own affairs. The last two groups began to hold services of their own, according to their own notions, thus defying the law that had established the prayer-book form of worship. This defiance of law on the part of these earnest people led the government to establish a special court, known as the Court of High Commission, to enforce the Act of Uniformity. But during the latter years of Elizabeth's reign the Puritans had gained so many sympathizers in the Privy Council and in Parliament that the act was not well enforced, and few were made to suffer because of their disobedience of the Act of Uniformity.

Laws against the Catholics.—Because of the many Catholic plots very stringent laws were passed against the Roman Catholics in Queen Elizabeth's time. In the first seventeen years of her reign, however, no one was put to death because of religion; but Catholic activity and political necessity forced religious persecution upon her. The Jesuits, a great Roman Catholic order formed in 1534–43 largely to combat Protestantism, became very active in England. They founded seminaries in northern France. There English priests were educated. At one of these seminaries—that at Douay—an English translation of the Bible known as the Douay version was made. Because of their activity all Jesuit and seminary priests were ordered to quit England, and any found harboring them were declared guilty of high treason. Then, finally, all Roman Catholics of the poorer class who dared proclaim their faith were banished, and the wealthier Catholics were not allowed to travel more than five miles from their homes.

James I and the Puritans.—When, on the death of Elizabeth in 1603, King James VI of Scotland became

James I of England, the extreme Protestants of England, especially the Presbyterians, hoped for a change in the affairs of the church, for the king had been raised a Calvinist and a Presbyterian; but their hopes were doomed to early disappointment, for at a great conference (held in 1604) known as the Hampton Court Conference, where church matters were discussed, King James declared against the Presbyterian form of church government. His motto was "No bishop, no king." He said, "Scotch presbytery—it agreeth as well with monarchy as God and the devil." He concluded a long speech before the conference with the ominous words, referring to the Puritans: "I will make them conform themselves or else I will harry them out of the land, or else do worse." There was, however, one great thing accomplished by this conference; for here a new translation of the English Bible was authorized and a group of scholars chosen to perform that task. This resulted in the great King James Version of the Bible, which made its appearance in 1611.

The religious motive in American colonization.—Thus we have seen how there arose groups of religious people in England who, because of their convictions, refused to obey the Act of Uniformity and thereby became subjects for persecution. The earliest of these groups to come to America were the Puritans, the first settling in Plymouth in 1620. They were soon followed by many thousands of others. By 1640 four Puritan colonies had been founded, and at least thirty thousand had migrated to America. Another great group to come to America because of religious persecution was the Quakers. They were cruelly persecuted in England during the reign of Charles II, and many thousands of them were thrown into prison. Finally, under their great benefactor, William Penn, they got the privilege of coming to America (1681), and here they established the colonies of Pennsylvania, New Jersey, and Delaware. Besides these larger bodies numerous smaller religious groups fled to America to gain freedom of religion. The Catholics fled from England to Maryland. Many German sects, such as the Mennonites, the Dunkers, the Moravians, and the Salzebergers, fled to

16

America for the same purpose, as did also the French Huguenots. The last great wave of immigration to America before the Revolution were the Scotch-Irish, who were also partly influenced by religious motives. Altogether, I think we may say truthfully, the religious motive was the strongest single motive in planting English colonies in America.

In the next chapter we will follow these various religious groups to America. We will try to understand how they organized their churches in the New World and what progress organized Christianity made there during the period we are accustomed to term the colonial period.

QUESTIONS FOR DISCUSSION

1. Is there any significance in the fact that the discovery of America and the beginning of the Protestant Reformation came within twenty-five years of each other?

2. What are some of the chief motives in colonization?

3. Would the English Reformation have occurred even if Henry VIII had not desired a divorce from Queen Catherine?

4. What were some of the earliest English translations of the Bible?

5. In what way did King Edward VI advance the cause of the English Reformation?

6. Why did Queen Mary Tudor remain a Catholic, and how did she attempt to restore Catholicism in England during her reign?

7. In what respect could we say that the English Reformation was completed during the reign of Queen Elizabeth?

8. How did the various groups of extreme Protestants arise in England, especially during the reigns of Elizabeth and James I?

9. How important was the religious motive in American colonization?

CHAPTER II

THE BEGINNING OF THE CHURCH IN THE COLONIES

THE story of the beginning of the church in America is closely related to the story of American colonization. We have already noticed how important was the religious motive in bringing colonists to America, and for our convenience here we may properly divide the colonists into religious groups as follows: (1) the Anglicans, or the members of the Church of England; (2) the Puritans, or Congregationalists; (3) the Friends, or Quakers; (4) the Presbyterians; and (5) the smaller colonial churches, such as the Catholics, Lutherans, Baptists, and Dutch Reformed.

The Church of England.—The three little ships that in 1607 brought the first permanent colonists to Jamestown, on the low-lying coasts of Virginia, brought also the germ of the Christian church. This colony was founded by a commercial company called the Virginia Company, which was made up largely of Puritan gentlemen. Composed of men of religious convictions, the company saw to it that the colonists were provided for, and from the beginning regular services were conducted. As long as Virginia was under the control of the company, Puritan ideas and Puritan clergymen had right of way, "low church" forms prevailed, and church attendance and Sabbath observance were strictly enforced. When Virginia became a royal colony, under the direct control of the crown, strong measures were taken to suppress nonconformity. Especially was this true of Sir William Berkeley, who became governor in 1641 and ruled for many years. In 1617 Governor Berkeley reported: "There are forty-eight parishes, and the ministers well paid. . . . But of all other commodities, so of this—the worst are sent us." All through the eighteenth century the government

18

of Virginia enforced uniformity of worship, though some French Huguenots and German exiles were admitted, and both were excepted from the Act of Uniformity. The few Baptists and Quakers in Virginia were persecuted and vilified, and, as a whole, religion remained at a low ebb in the colony through most of the seventeenth and eighteenth centuries.

The Established Church in Maryland.—As is well known, Maryland was founded by Lord Baltimore, a Catholic nobleman much interested in colonization. He was a member of both the New England and Virginia Companies and had previously made an attempt to establish a colony in Newfoundland. Much has been claimed for Lord Baltimore's religious toleration because he admitted both Catholics and Protestants to his colony, but certainly no credit is due the Catholic Church. The explanation of Lord Baltimore's toleration is that he was engaged in an immense land speculation, and nothing would have brought speedier ruin to his schemes than to have it suspected that he was governing his colony in the interests of the Catholics. As a matter of fact the Catholics were never in the majority in Maryland, and on the overthrow of King James II in 1688 the Church of England was established in Maryland, and the Catholics lost all political power. The type of ministers of the Church of England in Maryland was even worse than those in Virginia. The Established Church had no real government in the colony, and many of the ministers "hunted, raced horses, drank, gambled, and were the boon companions and parasites of the wealthy planters." The Maryland clergy became notorious and a byword in the other colonies. Whenever a clergyman got a bad reputation and was known as a low fellow he went under the name of a "Maryland parson." As a result of the corrupt state of the English Church in Maryland the dissenting churches made rapid headway, especially after the middle of the eighteenth century.

The English Church in other colonies.—The English Church was established in several of the other colonies, such as the Carolinas, Georgia, and New York, but it had a feeble growth and was never popular with the common people. The royal governors were of course members in most instances of the English Church and gave a certain official recognition to it—a fact that made it ever more obnoxious to the average colonist. Its support by the royal officials, however, gave it considerable political influence and prestige, and there were several fairly strong parishes in such cities as Philadelphia, New York, and other large towns. The Bishop of London had control of the Established Church in America. It was only through his appointment that clergymen could take a position in the colonies, for there was no resident American bishop during the colonial period. This was a great handicap, for candidates for the ministry had to go to England for ordination. Even more embarrassing was the fact that the rite of confirmation, which admits to membership in the English Church, could not be performed without a bishop; hence, few were admitted into the Established Church in colonial times. All through the eighteenth century there was agitation for the sending of a bishop to America, but there was always great opposition to such a move on the part of the dissenting people especially, who feared that an American bishop would attempt to interfere with their rights and religious privileges. The hatred of bishops was especially strong in New England, and to the continued agitation for a bishop on the part of the unpopular clergy of the English Church there may even be attributed one of the causes of the Revolution.

Missionaries from the Church in England.—The Society for the Propagation of the Gospel in Foreign Parts was an organization formed in 1701 by a group of Established churchmen in England for the purpose of raising money and sending missionaries to America. As a rule the men sent out by this society were of a far different type of men from the miserable incumbents in Virginia and Maryland. They did much to strengthen the English Church in New England, the middle colonies, and the Carolinas. Between 1702 and 1740 thirty-four missionaries were sent out by this society to North and South Carolina. It is interesting to recall that John Wesley served in Georgia under this organization.

20

The Puritan, or Congregational Church.—In many ways the most significant religious group of colonists coming to America in the seventeenth century were the Puritans. It is important to bear in mind that there were different kinds of Puritans. They were much divided among themselves in regard to details of doctrine, modes of worship, and ideas of church government. Out of these various differences came finally a number of sects. At the beginning of the colonizing period, however, there were two main kinds of Puritans: those who believed it better to stay in the Church of England and try to mold it according to their own views, and those who considered the English Church so hopelessly wrong that all Christians should withdraw from it. Both of these types came to America as colonists.

The Plymouth Colony.—The first group of Puritans to come to America were those who founded Plymouth in 1620. These were Separatists; that is, they had withdrawn from the Established Church. They had originally come from Scrooby, a little village in Nottinghamshire, England, not far from Epworth, where John Wesley was born. Here they were bitterly persecuted, and life became so intolerable to them that in 1608 they fled to Holland. In their flight from England they were hunted to the water's edge and only succeeded in escaping to Holland in scattered groups. At that time Holland was the only country in Europe where religious toleration prevailed. Finally, the congregation was united at Leyden, where it remained until 1620. After ten years of residence in Holland the leaders came to feel that they must leave, for they could not bear to live under foreign rule and see their children grow up and enter foreign service and perhaps fall away from the faith of their fathers. With this in mind they made arrangements to come to America. We are all familiar with the brave story of those first severe New England winters through which the Plymouth colony lived. Many died of their privations, but the brave-hearted few who remained kept the colony alive. Thus Plymouth became the mother of New England. At Plymouth a democratic form of government was established for both colony and church, and the Plymouth colonies were the founders of Congregationalism in America. The Plymouth settlers were few and poor, and their colony was soon overshadowed by the larger and richer Massachusetts Bay Colony; but they will always be remembered as pointing the way in which others were soon to follow.

The Massachusetts Bay Colony.—The next group of Puritans to come out to America were a very different kind from the poor and humble founders of Plymouth. They were Church of England men. In the years 1628 to 1629 they founded a group of towns about what is now Boston harbor. Said one of their ministers, "We do not come to New England as Separatists from the Church of England, though we cannot but separate from the corruptions in it." Though they had no intention of separating from the English church, it was not long after they had come to America before they had formed a church organization much like that of Plymouth. The three first ministers to come out, though already ordained in the Church of England, refused to accept their posts until they had been elected by the people, and then they were ordained as pastors of their little flocks, who had entered into a covenant, one with another, "to walk together before God according to his Word."

The Puritan congregations.—Beginning about 1630, English Puritans began to come to America in a great stream, and in ten years it is estimated that twenty thousand came out to New England. As church after church was organized, the example of the first congregation was followed. Each church was a self-governing unit and chose its own ministers. It was not long until church membership became a qualification for voting. It was considered the duty of the state to support the church, and all the people, whether church members or not, were taxed to support the ministers and required to attend the services. The strictest kind of Sabbath observance was enforced by law, and heretics were not only expelled from the church but banished from the colony. The minister was in many respects the most important and influential man in the community. The church was the central institution.

The Society of Friends, or Quakers.—Toward the close of the eighteenth century another great group of colonists, driven out of England by severe religious persecution, came to America and founded other colonies. These were the Friends, or Quakers. This sect had originated in England under the preaching of George Fox, who began his ministry about 1647. Fox taught that the final authority in religion was neither the Bible on the one hand nor the church on the other, but the Holy Spirit. He preached that the sacraments were not necessary. Priests and ministers who received salaries for their services were termed "hirelings." The Friends, or Quakers, conducted no formal service, but held simple meetings of believers, at which each man or woman spoke as the Spirit moved. Because of their seeming attack upon the church officials and apparent lack of respect for constituted authority the Quakers were looked upon much as we look upon the anarchists of to-day. For this reason they were persecuted not only in England, where thousands were thrown into prison, but in the colonies also.

The Quakers in Pennsylvania.—Fortunately for the Quakers, William Penn, son of a famous English admiral, was converted to their belief and joined the society. Because of his influential connections at court Penn was able to obtain a great grant of land in America in 1681. This the king insisted upon calling Pennsylvania. Here Penn proposed to found a colony that was to be open to all, even to Catholics and Jews, though unfortunately he was later compelled to exclude Catholics from holding office. Pennsylvania was the best-advertised of all the American colonies, and immediately the tide of immigration set in strongly not only from England, but from Holland, France, and especially Germany. To the colony came many sects besides the Quakers, such as Lutherans, Mennonites, and other peculiar German sects, besides French Protestants and Dutch Reformed adherents. Franklin estimated that one third of the people of colonial Pennsylvania were Quakers, one third Germans, and the remainder miscellaneous.

Presbyterianism.—The last great wave of immigrants to America before the Revolution was the Scotch-Irish.

Coming mostly from the north of Ireland, where they had immigrated during the reigns of Elizabeth and James I, the Scotch-Irish were Presbyterians and therefore subject to various disabilities in Ireland. They were forced to pay tithes to the Established Church of Ireland, and an Act passed in 1699, prohibiting the export of Irish woolens, led to great discontent among them. These were some of the reasons that started the wave of immigration to America. By 1720 they were swarming across the Atlantic. It has been estimated that they constituted the largest single element in the population of the colonies at the opening of the Revolution. In 1700 the Presbyterians were weak in the colonies, and their early ministers had been ordained by Scottish or Irish Presbyteries; but it was not long after the opening of the eighteenth century until they were organizing their own Presbyteries and ordaining their own ministers. Presbyterianism was strongest in the middle colonies, and there it was probably the most important religious element in the population. There were, in fact, several denominations that were Presbyterian in organization—the Dutch Reformed and the German Reformed Churches, as well as the Scotch-Irish Presbyterians. All these were found most numerously in New York and New Jersey. The first American Presbytery was organized in 1706 at Philadelphia. By 1758 several Presbyteries were united into the Synod of New York and Philadelphia. The Presbyterians were inclined toward a somewhat aggressive democracy and became a powerful factor in politics as well as in religion.

The smaller colonial churches.—The immigration of English Catholics to America during the colonial period was small except during the early years of the Maryland colony. Just before the Revolution a few Catholics from Ireland were beginning to come to America. The Catholics everywhere in the colonies were feared and regarded with suspicion by their Protestant neighbors, and there was little chance for them to develop before the Revolution. They did, however, build a few churches, including one in Philadelphia, where John Adams attended a service in 1774. The Baptists seem to have been considered the most radical of the dissenters during the colonial period. They were bitterly persecuted in most of the colonies, especially in New England, New York, and Virginia. There were a few scattered congregations in Rhode Island and Pennsylvania, but under the conditions prevailing large growth was impossible.

Religious intolerance.—In the early history of the American colonies there was little religious toleration. We have already noticed the intolerance in Virginia and in New England. It is interesting to notice that intolerance was strongest in those colonies in which church and state were most closely related. As time passed, various influences were at work to bring about religious toleration and the separation of church and state. Religious liberty found great advocates in such men as Roger Williams, William Penn, and Lord Baltimore, and the colonies they founded led the way in tolerance. Persecution for religious belief became less and less frequent. By the end of the colonial era it had almost disappeared.

We have attempted in this chapter to make clear the beginning of the church in America. In the next chapter we propose to discuss the Wesleyan revival in England and its extension to America in the latter half of the eighteenth century. The great American revival, which began about 1740, generally called *the Great Awakening,* was as important for America as the Wesleyan movement was for England. Out of this great American revival came not only a renewed religious life in the older churches but new religious forces, such as new educational foundations, and Methodism, which were destined to continue to influence America even down to our own day.

QUESTIONS FOR DISCUSSION

1. What were the most important religious groups to come to America during the colonial period?

2. In what colonies was the Church of England established? What was the type of clergymen sent out to the colonies by the Established Church?

3. What were some of the handicaps under which the English Church labored in America during the colonial period?

4. What was the Society for the Propagation of the

Gospel, and what was the nature of its work in America?

5. What is a Puritan? How many kinds of Puritans were there? What was the difference between the Puritans who founded Plymouth and those who established Massachusetts Bay Colony?

6. Tell of the great Puritan migration to America between 1630 and 1640. What were the various Puritan colonies founded in America?

7. Tell something of the origin of the Quakers, or Friends. How were they looked upon in England, and why were they so severely persecuted?

8. What was William Penn's position on toleration? Whom did Penn invite to his colonies?

9. In what colonies were the Presbyterians the most numerous? Where did the Scotch-Irish colonists come from, and where did they settle in America?

10. How numerous were the Baptists and the Catholics in the colonies? What were the several influences which tended to bring about religious toleration in the colonies?

CHAPTER III

THE WESLEYAN REVIVAL IN ENGLAND AND THE GREAT AWAKENING IN AMERICA

NEVER had the religious life of England been at a lower ebb than it was at the opening of the eighteenth century. The Reformation had spent its force, and the Established Church had settled down into a deathlike stupor, from which no power seemed able to awaken it. The church was degraded by its political connections, the bishops being simply political appointees who were as a rule hated by the lower clergy. Many of them lived outside of their dioceses and paid little attention to the affairs of the church. One Welsh bishop declared that he had never seen his diocese but once; others held numerous church offices at the same time and were interested only in the revenue from them. The majority of the lower clergy were poor and indolent, church buildings were out of repair, and the people were cold and indifferent to all religious matters. Said Montesquieu, the great French admirer of the English form of government, after one of his visits to England, "Everyone laughs if one talks of religion."

The prevalence of immorality and ignorance.—Knowing that such were the religious conditions, we are not surprised that drunkenness and immorality were everywhere prevalent. Even the most prominent statesmen were known for the grossness of their lives. It was the custom of Walpole, the prime minister, to tell his son at the dinner table to drink two glasses of wine to his one, because he did not want the son to see his father under the table. One of the prime ministers was accustomed to appear at the play accompanied by his mistress, while the courts of the first two Georges were notorious for their vileness. Says the historian Green, "Purity and fidelity to the marriage vow was sneered out of fashion."

Conditions among the poor.—If vileness and immorality were common among the upper classes, they were even more so among the great masses of the poor. Never had the life of the poor of England been so brutalized, and never were poverty, ignorance, and filth more prevalent than among the submerged classes of eighteenth-century England. There was no attempt on the part of the church to reach the poorer classes, neither were there schools for them; and the poor laws passed in the reign of Queen Elizabeth tended to create rather than eliminate pauperism. The criminal laws were extremely severe, there being more than two hundred crimes punishable by death. But instead of decreasing, crime was steadily on the increase, and "society was constantly in terror of violent mobs, which broke out continually in London and Birmingham, burning houses, opening jails, plundering and pillaging at will." Cheap new intoxicants such as rum and gin gave a new impetus to drunkenness among the poor. The gin shops of the towns and cities invited passers-by to get drunk for a penny, dead drunk for two pence, with clean straw provided for nothing. From descriptions of the life of the times it would seem that that invitation was frequently accepted.

Prison conditions.—Prison conditions were horrible past belief. The jailers bought their places and received their pay through fees. As a result they were little more than extortioners. Prisoners acquitted of the crime for which they had been arrested were often dragged back to prison because of the fees they owed the jailers. Criminals of all classes were huddled together, no separation was provided for the sexes, every jail was infested with vermin, and brutality to prisoners was the common rule.

The Holy Club at Oxford.—The movement that, more than any other, was destined to change the life of England began among a group of earnest students in attendance upon the ancient University of Oxford. These young men were studying for the priesthood in the Church of England and were stanch churchmen; but they were disturbed by the deadness of the religious life about them. They met, at first, regularly for prayer, but they soon broadened their activities to visiting the prisons and in

28

other ways attempted to reach the poor and outcast all about them. Their methodical regularity of life soon gained for them the nickname "Methodists," given them at first in derision. Several of this group, after their Oxford days were over, continued their work among the poor, which they had begun in the quiet university town, and it was not long before they were attracting public attention. The three outstanding members of this Holy Club were the two brothers John and Charles Wesley, the sons of Samuel Wesley, a clergyman of the Church of England, and George Whitefield, a charity student at Pembroke College, son of a tavern keeper.

Characteristics of the three Methodist founders.—These three religious enthusiasts possessed qualifications ideally suited for the inauguration of a great religious revival. Whitefield was above everything else a preacher. Charles Wesley was one of those sweet spirits gifted in the writing of religious poetry and became the sweet singer of the movement. He did much to tone the extravagant features of the revival by setting the converts to singing his chaste and beautiful lines. John Wesley was the outstanding organizer, though in power as a preacher he stood next to Whitefield. As a hymn writer he ranks next to his brother. His greatest work, however, was in his ability to combine all the best elements of the movement. By devising rules and organization he was able through the Methodist movement to offer a permanent contribution not alone to the religious life of the eighteenth century, but to the religious life of the world.

The Wesleyan Revival in England.—The Wesleyan Revival may be said to have begun in the year 1737, when this little group of Oxford students removed to London and began the work of carrying religion and morality to the masses. "Their voice was soon heard in the wildest and most barbarous corners of the land, among the bleak moors of Northumberland, or in the dens of London, or on the long galleries, where in the pauses of their labor the Cornish miners listened to the sobbing of the sea." Never had England heard such preaching; never had England witnessed such results. Whitefield, with his sympathy for the sin and sorrow of mankind and with his marvelous voice, soon had a following among the poor and the admiration of many among the mighty. Preaching to twenty thousand miners grimy from the coal pits at Kingswood, he brought a message that reached the hearts of those hardened men; and as he preached he could see their tears making white channels down their blackened faces. It was from Whitefield that John Wesley learned to preach in the fields, for the pulpits of the English Church were soon closed against them. It was not long until opponents arose, and the early Methodist preachers were mobbed, stoned, and ducked, and their lives often endangered. But on they went, carrying the message of a regenerate life until thousands were overtaken by a terrible sense of conviction for sin, a dread of hell, and "a new hope of heaven."

The first Methodist society.—Methodism as an organization dates from the year 1739, when John Wesley drew up for his society in London a set of rules for the regulation and control of their religious life and activities. Other societies were rapidly formed, adopting Wesley's rules. Soon Wesley found himself engaged in traveling over England, Scotland, Wales, and Ireland, visiting his societies, which were soon formed into circuits and Conferences. By about the middle of the century we find him making annual tours to all parts of the United Kingdom. Forty-two times he visited Ireland, and year by year we find him touring Scotland and Wales, but still spending much of his time in England. Although traveling from four to six thousand miles a year, he found time to read and write, and his numerous books and tracts on many subjects did much to further the cause and spread intelligence among the lowly, among whom Methodism found its first great success.

The early Methodist movement.—It must be kept in mind that the early Methodist revival was a movement within the Church of England. In fact, the Wesleys never thought of English Methodism in any other light. Its best preachers were all ministers in the Established Church, although lay preaching was soon adopted as a Methodist practice. Indeed, I think it proper to say that the English Church broke away from the Methodist societies rather than that the Methodists broke away from the church. It was not until after Wesley's death that the final break with the English Church came. Within that church there developed, however, a strong evangelical party, which in the next century gained dominance and was largely responsible for bringing new life into the state church.

Results of the Wesleyan revival.—When Wesley died at the age of eighty-eight, the Methodists numbered more than a hundred thousand. Since that time they have gone on increasing not alone in England, but especially in America, becoming one of the great religious forces in the world. But the formation of a new and militant church was not the only result of this great movement. As we have already seen, its effect upon the English church was marked. It made the absentee bishop and the fox-hunting parson impossible. The revival was responsible for a new moral enthusiasm in England, which not alone affected the religious life, but stopped the nefarious trade in slaves, cleaned up the terrible prison conditions, established the Sunday school, built new hospitals, sent out missionaries to foreign lands, reformed the English public schools, raised the status of the agricultural laborer, and brought about the reform of the English Parliament.

Whitefield the connecting link.—While the Wesleyan revival was getting under way in England, a similar movement was beginning in the colonies. Absolutely separate in their origin, the two movements were finally connected through the work of George Whitefield, who came to America several times, traveled through the colonies on extended preaching tours, and came to have the largest influence of any of the revival preachers in America.

The beginning of the Great Awakening in America.—What is generally known as the Great Awakening began at Northampton, Massachusetts, under the preaching of Jonathan Edwards, an extremely able Congregational minister, in the winter of 1734. In a series of sermons in which the doctrine of justification by faith alone was set forth very strongly Edwards so impressed the people in and about Northampton that soon religious concern was everywhere evident. Before the winter was over, more than three hundred had professed conversion. This was only the beginning of a religious awakening that swept throughout the New England colonies. From Northampton it spread to other towns in the Connecticut valley, and places as far away as New Haven felt its effect. News of the movement was printed and circulated in England. Nor was this movement over in a year. The revivalist preachers continued their efforts through several years and were greatly aided by the coming to America of the greatest revivalist of the century—George Whitefield. Nor was the revival confined to New England, for in the middle colonies a similar movement was begun, especially among the German and Dutch Reformed and Presbyterian Churches, which in many ways was even more fruitful in results than the New England revival.

Some results of the New England revival.—The great revival brought new life to the Congregational churches of New England. However, the enthusiasm aroused by the revival displeased many of the more conservative, and it was not long until a division arose. Many congregations that favored the revival broke away from Congregationalism and became Baptist churches. Another effect of the revival manifested itself in a reaction against some of the main doctrines of old-time Calvinism, such as original sin, predestination, and even the doctrine of the Trinity. This latter movement culminated later in the Unitarian movement, which began to take shape after the Revolution.

The revival in the middle colonies.—The outstanding names in connection with the revival in the middle colonies are William Tennent and his four sons. The elder Tennent had been a minister in the Church of Ireland, but on coming to America he left the Established Church and became a minister in the Presbyterian Church. Having been educated in the University of Glasgow, Tennent undertook the education of his four sons. His study soon became a school, where not only his sons but other students were received. Better to accommodate his students he built a log house, which was called in derision "Log College." From this Log College went out sixteen graduates, whose work as educators and preachers gives ample testimony to the thoroughness of the elder Tennent's instruction. It was this group of students, graduates of the

Log College, who formed the nucleus of what later became the evangelical party within the Presbyterian Church. New Brunswick, New Jersey, where Gilbert Tennent was minister, was the geographical center of the revival among Presbyterians; but the several middle colonies soon felt its influence.

The revival among the Dutch Reformed churches.— Meanwhile a revival was in progress among the Dutch Reformed churches under the leadership of Theodorus J. Frelinghuysen, who had been sent from Holland to be pastor of the Dutch Reformed church at Raritan, New Jersey. His preaching had been from the beginning of an evangelistic nature, and it was not long before the revival fire had penetrated into all the churches in the region. Frelinghuysen's independence and liberality soon alienated, however, the more conservative among the Dutch Reformed adherents, and two parties arose among them, such as had arisen in New England among the Congregationalists. One favored the revival and the revival methods, and the other was strong in opposition. The same parties had also arisen among the Presbyterians.

We have noticed the coming of new life to several of the churches in America through the preaching of Jonathan Edwards, Frelinghuysen, and the Tennents, with their associates: let us now see how all these independent movements were united into one great intercolonial revival.

George Whitefield and his preaching tours in America. We have seen that George Whitefield had been a member of the Holy Club at Oxford and that he had achieved great fame as a preacher in England. In 1739 he was induced to come to America. Landing in Delaware, he began at once a tireless evangelistic tour of the colonies. Everywhere he was received with great rejoicing by the several evangelistic groups in the Presbyterian, the Dutch Reformed, the German Reformed, and the Lutheran Churches. Even in the Established Church were found many who welcomed his message. In New England the way was made ready for him by Edwards' revival. Everywhere vast crowds flocked to hear him. Many who were members of no church, such as Benjamin Franklin, be-

came his stanch supporters. Seven times Whitefield
visited America, preaching from Georgia to New England,
and literally wore himself out for America; for soon after
he landed on his visit of 1770 he was taken ill. When
urged to rest he remarked, "I had rather wear out than
rust out," and soon after, he died at Newburyport, Massachusetts, where to-day his body lies buried. Whitefield's
great work for America was in uniting the evangelical
forces of the colonies into one great intercolonial movement; and when independence came a few years after his
death, the churches of America were vigorously alive, ready
to take their full part in the building of the new nation.

The educational influence of the Great Awakening.—
The Great Awakening gave a tremendous impulse to education. As gifted young men were led into the Christian
life, the ministers began to bestir themselves to provide
educational facilities to prepare them to preach the gospel.
Thus were created the College of New Jersey at Princeton,
Queen's College at New Brunswick, Dartmouth in New
Hampshire, and Brown at Providence. The great hall
erected for George Whitefield in Philadelphia became a
charity school—a school that later developed into the
University of Pennsylvania.

**The relation of the Great Awakening to the American
Revolution.—**There can be readily traced an intimate connection between the American Revolution and this great
intercolonial revival of religion. The revivalists of all
denominations stood for cooperation and advocated union.
It was indeed the first intellectual and emotional movement in which all the colonies participated. The evangelical churches ignored colonial boundaries and built
"constituencies which were intercolonial in character." The
churches that were greatly strengthened by the revival,
such as the Presbyterian and Baptist, were unanimous on
patriotic questions. The revival churches also stood for
separation of church and state—a principle that gloriously
triumphed a few years later, when our constitutional
fathers met to form "a more perfect union."

QUESTIONS FOR DISCUSSION

1. Describe religious conditions in England at the open-

ing of the eighteenth century. Describe social and moral conditions at the same time.

2. What was the Holy Club, and why did its members get the nickname "Methodists"?

3. Who were the three great leaders of early Methodism, and what were their individual characteristics?

4. Describe the nature of the Methodist revival in England and tell of the formation of the first society.

5. What were the outstanding results of the Wesleyan revival in England?

6. When and where did the Great Awakening begin in America, and what were some of the results in New England?

7. Tell of the Great Awakening in the middle colonies? Who were the chief leaders there? What was the "Log College"?

8. Describe the preaching tours of George Whitefield in America. What was the effect of his preaching and his work upon the American churches?

9. What were some of the educational influences of the Great Awakening?

10. What was the relation of the Great Awakening to the American Revolution?

CHAPTER IV

THE AMERICAN CHURCHES DURING AND FOLLOWING THE REVOLUTION

If it were possible to find statistics showing the attitude of the American churches toward the Revolution, they would undoubtedly show that the Congregationalists of New England and the Presbyterians of the middle colonies, and especially the Scotch-Irish Presbyterians in the back country, were on the whole the most devoted to the cause of independence. Naturally the English Church, being the state church, was closely connected with the executive government of the colonies and contained large numbers of loyalists. The small group of Methodists then in the colonies were also suspected of loyalist sympathies, for as yet they were a part of the Church of England, and John Wesley was stanch in his support of George III and the cause of the English government. The Catholics were few in number and had little part in winning independence, though the recent Irish immigrants were naturally hostile to England, and the Maryland Catholics were generally favorable to independence. The smaller colonial churches, such as the Baptists, the Lutherans, and the Dutch and German Reformed, contained numbers of patriots. This was especially true of those congregations in which the recent religious awakening had been effective.

Effect of the Revolutionary War upon the churches.— Of all the churches in America the Established Church suffered most, because of the large loyalist element among its membership. The Methodists likewise were under suspicion, and in several of the States, as in Maryland, their preachers were persecuted and imprisoned because of their supposed loyalist sympathies. The Methodist missionary Francis Asbury, however, had remained in America throughout the war, and the membership of the

Methodist societies increased in spite of persecution. The Presbyterians and the Baptists came out of the struggle with increased prestige; and when peace came, they occupied with the Congregationalists of New England the most advantageous position.

The new Constitution and religious liberty.—In several colonies, as we will remember, there had been an established church, as in Virginia, Maryland, and the Carolinas, where the Church of England was the state church; and in Connecticut and Massachusetts, where the Congregational Church was largely supported by the state. When the colonies became States and formed new constitutions, the idea of a state church was not entirely eliminated, and complete separation of church and state was not everywhere accomplished. Concessions, however, were made to dissenters, and as a whole there was much more religious liberty than formerly. In 1785 Virginia passed a law declaring that no Virginian could henceforth be compelled to attend or support any form of religious worship; but in Massachusetts and Connecticut complete separation of the church from the state did not take place until the nineteenth century. Gradually the cause of religious liberty was everywhere victorious, and there was finally written into the fundamental law of the land the declaration, "Congress shall make no law respecting the establishment of religion or prohibiting the free exercise thereof."

Reorganization of the American churches.—During the period of the colonies several of the American churches had been governed from England. Thus, the Bishop of London had control of the Established Church in the colonies; the Vicar-Apostolic in London directed the affairs of the American Catholics; and John Wesley exercised complete control over the American Methodists. In each of these cases political independence meant also ecclesiastical independence. Bishops were ordained for America in the Established Church, and in 1789 these churches were organized as the Protestant Episcopal Church in the United States. In the same year John Carroll, of Maryland, was ordained a bishop—the first Roman Catholic bishop in the United States. In 1788 the Presbyterians organized a General Assembly for the United States. The churches with the congregational form of church government, such as the Baptist, the Lutheran, and the Congregational, were already independent of European control. The Methodist was the first American church, among those which had been controlled from England, to become independent of that control. John Wesley, then very aged, devised a plan for the separation of the American Methodists from his own control, and at a Conference held in Baltimore in 1784 this plan was adopted, and the Methodist Episcopal Church was formed, with Dr. Thomas Coke and Francis Asbury as general superintendents.

American Christianity following independence.—One of the outstanding characteristics of American Christianity following the gaining of independence was the rapid growth and extension of what might be termed the popular and democratic churches. The churches that more than any others attempted to meet the peculiar needs of the new communities in America were the Baptist, the Methodist, and the Presbyterian. Perhaps the reason for the more rapid extension of these three churches was the fact that they were considered more democratic than the older churches of the seaboard; therefore, they made a larger appeal, especially to the American frontiersman.

Movement of population westward.—No sooner was the Revolution over than population began to move westward over the mountains, and many new communities were soon to be found in the valleys of the streams flowing into the Ohio. Thus Kentucky and Tennessee were occupied and ready for Statehood by 1792 and 1796 respectively. Ohio, Indiana, Illinois, Alabama, and Mississippi applied for admission as States only a few years later. It was in these new States and among the frontier settlements that the three great democratic churches already mentioned were to gain their first great victories.

Frontier conditions and the churches.—The Baptist and Presbyterian Churches early gained large followings in the new West, though in their organization they lacked some of the advantages of the Methodist circuit system. Their ministers were generally settled in one community, serving never more than two or three congregations at most. To provide for the support of a settled pastor a congregation would need to be fairly large, and many of the smaller Presbyterian and Baptist churches in the West were frequently without pastors and regular preaching. In the Methodist circuit system a preacher served not one community but numerous communities. In a new country, where settlements were few and far between, the circuits were sometimes as large as four hundred miles around, and the preacher occupied from four to six weeks in making the rounds of his circuit. Thus each Methodist preacher covered a very large territory. Another factor that made the Methodist Church peculiarly adaptable to frontier conditions was the use of lay, or local preachers. A young man who showed any ability in public speaking was urged by the circuit rider to exercise his gifts on every possible occasion, and when the presiding elder came round to hold the Quarterly Conference, the young man was recommended for an exhorter's license. Later, if he was found worthy, he was granted a local preacher's license. As a rule, however, the local preacher did not travel a circuit, but preached in his own and neighboring communities, often organizing new classes in frontier settlements before the regular circuit preacher appeared on the scene.

The democratic churches on the frontier.—By 1800 the three principal frontier churches were well established in the West. Then the Presbyterians had at least seven presbyteries in Kentucky and Tennessee and along the upper Ohio and at least seven other presbyteries in western North and South Carolina, Virginia, and Pennsylvania. At the same time there were nine Baptist associations in Kentucky, Tennessee, and Ohio, and five other associations in the western sections of the older States. The Methodists were well established in the same region with two districts and thirteen circuits in Kentucky, Tennessee, and Ohio; and the western sections of the older States were covered with a network of circuits and districts. In Kentucky alone in 1800 there were 106 Baptist churches and more than 5,000 members. In Tennessee the Baptists were early on the ground and were probably the most numerous of any religious denomination in the West. In 1815 there were about 60 Presbyterian congregations in Tennessee and about 25 ministers. In 1811 there were 17,511 white Methodists in Kentucky and Tennessee, and 1,415 colored; the total membership of the Methodists in the West in the same year being 30,740.

The great revival in the West, 1797—1805.—The outstanding event in the early history of the churches on the frontier in the closing years of the eighteenth and the opening years of the nineteenth century was a great religious revival, which began in Kentucky in 1797 and continued with little interruption until about 1805. This movement had its beginning among the Presbyterians in Kentucky, but soon spread to other religious groups. Eventually it greatly influenced all the frontier churches. One of the features of the revival was the spirit of cooperation and toleration which existed among the various churches. One great camp-meeting assembly was described as made up of all denominations. Presbyterians, Methodists, and Baptists were in full and hearty communion with one another. The meetings were often attended by great emotional excitement. People under conviction fell to the ground unconscious, as if shot by a rifle, and such strange exercises as "the shakes" were common manifestations. These strange phenomena were not peculiar to one group, but were found among Baptists, Methodists, and Presbyterians alike.

Origin of the camp meeting.—An institution that had its origin in the West during the great revival—an institution that has exercised a great historic influence—is the camp meeting. Originally used by the Presbyterians in Kentucky, it found its chief development among the Methodists. Within a few years a camp meeting was conducted on practically every circuit in the West. It became a frontier institution of great social and religious importance. Camp meetings, held in the woods, attracted people for miles around. Whole families came with their simple effects for a week's outing and lived in booths and tents, enjoying delightful seasons of religious and social intercourse with others like-minded. Not alone did the religious come, but the irreligious as well: the young frontier rowdies, the hucksters selling whisky and other wares, all were attracted; and many times the preachers had great difficulty in keeping order and in preventing the rough element from breaking up their meetings. In 1811 Bishop Asbury estimated that between four hundred and five hundred camp meetings were held annually by the Methodist Church. By 1818 the institution had been brought to northern Ohio and western New York, and in that year a camp meeting was held for the first time on the "Chetauqua" circuit, undoubtedly the forerunner of the modern Chautauqua.

Results of the Western revival.—The immediate fruits of the great Western revival were reaped largely by the Methodists and Baptists, for the Presbyterians suffered serious schisms. The two most serious of these disruptions from the Presbyterian Church were the Cumberland Presbyterian Church and the Disciples of Christ, or the Christian Church. These two new churches were formed largely because of the failure of the Presbyterians to meet the peculiar demands of the frontier. Many of the influential ministers of the Presbyterian Church were greatly concerned about the "excesses" of the revival, with the result that certain of the more active of the revivalist ministers were suspended. Another problem arising out of the revival was the difficulty of obtaining ministers in sufficient numbers to meet the increased needs. To meet the demand for more ministers certain presbyteries lowered the educational standards for ordination. This act was severely condemned by many of the more conservative, for the Presbyterians had prided themselves on their educated ministry. As a result of this difference of opinion a group of ministers formed themselves into a separate presbytery, which developed into the Cumberland Presbyterian Church. This new denomination continued to practice the methods developed by the revival. At the same time its ministers preached a milder Calvinism. The Disciples of Christ drew largely from the Presbyterians. Both Baptists and Methodists, however, greatly increased their membership; for they were more successful in adapting revival methods to their usual mode of working.

Frontier preaching.—A peculiar type of preaching developed on the frontier. It was extemporaneous in style and dealt largely with future rewards and punishments. All denominations emphasized the Adamic fall and laid stress on the necessity of conversion. The present general conception of frontier preaching seems to be that it was wild and incoherent, with little that appealed to thinking people. This may have been true of some, but it hardly can be called characteristic. The preachers were often noisy and vigorous, but most of them had regard for the decencies of public worship and did not encourage the extravagant. If a preacher wished to have any influence in a frontier community he had to preach without manuscript. Many of the New England missionaries sent out by the Congregationalists used manuscripts in their discourses, and of them the Methodists especially had a poor opinion. Peter Cartwright gave this advice to one such missionary: "I told him to quit reading his old manuscript sermons and learn to speak extemporaneously; that the Western people were born and reared in hard times and were an outspoken and offhand people; that if he did not adopt this manner of preaching the Methodists would set the whole Western world on fire before he could light his match." The great mass of the Western people, according to Cartwright, "wanted a preacher that could mount a stump or a block or a log, or stand in the bed of a wagon, and, without notes or manuscript, quote, expound; and apply the Word of God to the heart and consciences of the people."

Education and the frontier preacher.—Schools had little to do with the making of the frontier preacher. There was not a single college graduate in the Indiana Conference of the Methodist Church until the forties, and the total number of college-bred men in the whole Methodist Church in the West at the same time could have been counted on the fingers of both hands. This was largely true of the Baptists and Cumberland Presbyterians also, though the regular Presbyterians clung to their high educational standards for the ministry—a requirement that very probably kept the Presbyterians from developing many outstanding preachers of the frontier type. Many of the most successful preachers of the West were uneducated men, but they were uneducated in the same sense in which Abraham Lincoln was uneducated: like Lincoln they read few books, but they were thoughtful and devoted to the work they considered the most important in the world.

The beginning of modern missions.—The settlement of the American frontier and the pushing of the churches westward had a great influence upon the beginning of the modern missionary movement. The first missionaries sent out by the American churches were those sent among the Indians. The best known of these early missionaries was John Eliot, pastor at Roxbury, Massachusetts, who began his work among the Indians in 1646 and continued it with zeal and success until his death in 1690. Through his efforts numerous Indian churches were formed. Before his death twenty-four Indian preachers were proclaiming the gospel. Through his influence the Society for the Propagation of the Gospel in New England was formed in 1649, which was the first missionary society in America. The earliest Presbyterian missionary was David Brainerd (died 1790), who began work among the Indians in 1743 —a work that was continued after the Revolution. The Methodists began their missionary efforts in Ohio among the Wyandot Indians in 1817, the first Methodist worker being a mulatto—John Stewart. In 1819, due to the interest aroused over the work among the Wyandots, a Methodist Missionary Society was formed. The great religious needs of the new West following the Revolution brought home to the American churches, as nothing else had done, the necessity for missionary endeavor, and soon numerous missionaries were at work west of the Alleghanies.

The beginning of foreign missions.—An event of great importance in the history of American Christianity is the beginning of interest in foreign missions. Williams College has the honor of being the mother of the American foreign-missionary movement, for it was among a group of Williams College students that the leaven of foreign missions began its work. Samuel John Mills, who entered Williams College in 1809, was the center of a group of praying students who caught a vision of the need of carrying Christianity to foreign fields. These students sent an appeal to the church to send them out as missionaries, and in response the American Board of Commissioners for Foreign Missions was organized in 1811. Four years later the Baptists formed their first Missionary Society in order to support Adoniram Judson and Luther Rice, two members of Mills' band who had become Baptists after they had sailed for India. It was thus that the great modern foreign-missionary movement was inaugurated.

QUESTIONS FOR DISCUSSION

1. What religious groups in America contained the largest numbers of patriots, and why?

2. Why were Methodists under suspicion during the Revolution?

3. What does our Constitution say about the separation of church and state?

4. How were the churches reorganized after the winning of independence—especially the Episcopal, the Methodist, and the Presbyterian?

5. What were the three churches that may be termed the democratic churches?

6. Explain the peculiar conditions of the frontier that confronted the churches in their attempts to spread Christianity in the West.

7. Tell of the great Western revival (1795—1805) and its effect upon the Baptists, the Methodists, and the Presbyterians especially.

8. What was the origin of the camp meeting, and what part did it play on the frontier?

9. Describe the outstanding peculiarities of frontier preaching.

10. Tell something of the beginning of missionary work among the Indians.

11. Where did the foreign-missionary movement begin in America? When were the first American foreign-missionary societies organized?

CHAPTER V

TYPES OF CHURCH GOVERNMENT

In the long course of the history of the Christian Church at least four types of church government have developed: the papal, the episcopal, the presbyterian, and the congregational. Practically all the churches in the world may be said to have one or another of these four kinds of church government or a combination of two or more of the types. In discussing these various kinds of church governments or polities we will make no attempt to uphold one kind as against another, nor will we try to show which has been the most successful or is the most scriptural; our aim will be simply to explain the theory on which each type rests and then to give a brief description of church government as it is carried on under each type.

The papal type.—We will begin our study with an examination of the papal type of church government. This type of church government is perhaps the most important, since it was the first to become fully developed in the Western world and has perhaps exercised a longer and larger influence than any of the others.

The papal theory of church government.—The theory upon which papal church government is based is briefly as follows: The Roman Catholic Church is "the mother and mistress of all churches" and is therefore the only true Church of Christ. The jurisdiction over this only true church was expressly given by Christ himself to the apostle Peter, and the power that was given to Peter by Jesus has remained in the hands of Peter's successors —the bishops of Rome, or the Popes—from that time until now. This Roman bishop, or the Pope, as we commonly call him, when he speaks *ex cathedra*—that is, when he speaks as the head of the church—regarding faith and morals, is absolutely infallible, because he speaks as God's representative.

The scriptural basis for this theory.—The scriptural basis for this theory of the church may be summed up briefly as follows: "That they all may be one; as thou, Father, *art* in me, and I in thee, that they also may be one in us. . . ." (John 17. 21, King James Version). Perhaps the most important Scripture reference supporting this theory is the words of Jesus found in Matt. 16. 17-19. In his conversation with Peter, Jesus says: "Blessed art thou, Simon Bar-Jonah: for flesh and blood hath not revealed it unto thee, but my Father who is in heaven. And I also say unto thee, that thou art Peter, and upon this rock I will build my church; and the gates of Hades shall not prevail against it. I will give unto thee the keys of the kingdom of heaven: and whatsoever thou shalt bind on earth shall be bound in heaven; and whatsoever thou shalt loose on earth shall be loosed in heaven." This passage seems to be a strong support of the papal theory, but we find that Christ gave the same power to all the apostles (John 20. 23), and what is given to all can hardly be made to apply to one only. This would seem to be a slender basis for such an elaborate system as the papal system of church government, but we must bear in mind that the Roman Catholic does not consider the Bible in the same way as does the Protestant Church. He places the authority of tradition at least on a par with the Bible, and the decrees of councils and Popes are to him equally authoritative with the Scriptures. It goes, then, without saying that the chief basis for the papal theory of the church is to be found in the decrees of councils and in tradition rather than in the Bible.

How the Roman Catholic Church is governed.—There is only one church that adheres to the papal theory of church government, and that is the Roman Catholic. Its government is monarchial. More than that, it is absolute, the Pope being the supreme and absolute ruler. The members of the Roman Catholic Church have no part whatever in its government. Below the Pope are the cardinals (appointed by the Pope), who act as an advisory council, but whose every decision may be changed and revised by the Pope. Subject to the papal authority are the bishops, who preside over districts called dioceses. The priests minister to the people who are gathered into congregations. There are adjunctive agents, such as monks and nuns, having no part in the government of the church, and presided over by their own officials. All the property of the Roman Catholic Church is held in trust and is controlled by the bishops, and not by the local congregations.

The papacy historically developed.—The Roman Catholics claim that the apostle Peter was the first Pope and ruled as such in Rome. For this claim, however, there is no historic proof. At first the Bishop of Rome had no more authority than had any other bishop; but very gradually, because Rome was the capital of the Roman Empire and the most important city in the West, the Bishop of Rome came to be considered as the most important official in the Western church. He naturally was frequently called upon, because of his position in the capital, to settle disputes outside his own jurisdiction, and little by little he came to be looked upon as the head of the whole Western church. Historians generally agree in saying that Pope Leo I (449) was the first Pope in anything like the modern sense; that is, he was the first Roman bishop actually to exercise authority over the whole Western church. It is important to bear in mind, however, that the Eastern, or Greek Church never fully recognized the authority of the Roman Pope; for in the East the Bishops of Alexandria, Antioch, Constantinople, and Jerusalem considered themselves as important as the Bishop of Rome. Finally, the Eastern and Western churches were completely separated, very largely over the question of papal supremacy.

The episcopal theory of church government.—The episcopal theory is older than the papal theory of church government, for the church in Jerusalem was the mother church, and not the Roman church. The origin of the episcopal theory can be easily traced. In the primitive or New Testament churches there was a body of officials known as elders, or, to use the Greek term, *presbyters.* When this body met, it was presided over by one of its own number, and this presiding official came to be called a bishop, though in the New Testament the bishop is undoubtedly simply an elder appointed to preside over the body of elders. Gradually the bishop came to stand above the other elders of the local church, for every church at first had its presiding elder, or bishop. Sometimes the elders of several neighboring churches would meet for consultation, and the bishop of the largest church or the church in the largest city would be chosen to preside. In the interim between meetings he would be called upon to settle questions or would be frequently asked for advice by the others. Thus there arose an official whose duty it was to look after the affairs of a group of churches, and he retained the title of bishop.

The principal element in the episcopal theory.—The principal element in the episcopal theory of the church is what is known as "apostolic succession." That is, the ministry, to be valid, must be in unbroken succession from the apostles. No minister, according to this theory, can be truly ordained and have authority to administer the sacraments unless he is ordained by some bishop who himself has been ordained by one who is in an unbroken line of succession from the apostles. This theory holds that the life of the church can be preserved and handed down only through the apostolic succession of her ministry. Any church, therefore, is a true branch of the Catholic Church whose ministry is in apostolic succession. "The touch of a bishop's fingers in succession is the essential principle, since neither faith nor worship nor works avail anything without this official touch."

The episcopal system of church government.—The episcopal system of church government must have different orders of the clergy, such as deacons, priests, bishops, archbishops, and patriarchs; but all these are not necessary to the system. Each order of the ministry must have its own sphere of action in order to prevent confusion; hence, the bishop has his diocese, and the priest his parish or congregation. There are national conventions, or convocations, generally composed of two houses. Into the lower house laymen may be admitted. The convention, or convocation, has authority to determine matters of faith, discipline, ritual, and worship, though it must do nothing that contradicts the Scriptures. The bishop has the sole power to confirm members into the church and to ordain to holy orders. No one not thus officially ordained by a bishop can preside over a congregation.

Types of episcopal churches.—The oldest episcopal church in the world is the Catholic and Apostolic Church of the East, commonly called the Greek Church. This church recognizes three orders of the clergy, deacons, priests, and bishops, though it has patriarchs; but these patriarchs are of the order of bishops, and not a separate order. The Anglican, or Established Church of England, dating from the reign of Henry VIII, is also an episcopal church, as is the Protestant Episcopal Church in the United States.

The presbyterian type.—The presbyterian form of church government is older than either the episcopal or the papal, though it was later in development. As we have already noticed, the primitive churches had a group of elders in each, who ruled the church and were called a "presbytery." We have seen how this early presbytery developed into the episcopal, and the episcopal into the papal form of church government. The presbyterian form as we know it to-day is of much later development.

Modern Presbyterianism.—Modern Presbyterianism dates from John Calvin, the great reformer. It was Calvin's aim to formulate a form of church government which would prevent the disintegration of the Protestant forces and at the same time match the power and efficiency of Rome. Calvin's scheme of church polity was put into operation at Geneva, Switzerland. From there it spread throughout southern Germany into Holland, was taken into Scotland by John Knox, spread from Scotland into north Ireland, and from all these various sources it was brought to America.

Presbyterian theory and practice.—According to the presbyterian theory of the church there are two kinds of elders in the New Testament: ministerial, or preaching, and ruling, or lay elders. The bodies that rule the church are (1) the session, (2) the presbytery, (3) the synod, and (4) the assembly. The session is made up of ruling and preaching elders and is the governing body of the congregation. This body admits, disciplines, and dismisses members and also elects from itself delegates, or commissioners, to the higher bodies—the presbytery and the synod. The presbytery consists of all the ministers and one ruling elder from each congregation within a certain district. It has power to receive appeals from church sessions; to examine and approve or censure, install, remove, and judge ministers; to examine and approve or censure the records of church sessions; to determine questions of doctrine and discipline and to unite or divide churches at the request of the people or to form new congregations. The next higher body is the synod, which must be composed of at least three presbyteries. It has power to receive appeals from presbyteries and forms, unites, or divides them. The synod also has the power to propose legislation to the general assembly. The general assembly is the governing body of the church. Its membership is made up of an equal number of ministerial and lay elders. It has the power to receive appeals, to examine records of synods, to decide matters regarding doctrine and discipline, to erect new synods, and to superintend the concerns of the whole church.

The presbyterian churches.—There are a large number of churches having the presbyterian form of church polity, not only in the United States but also in Europe. The best-known presbyterian churches in the United States are the various branches of the Presbyterian Church proper, the German Reformed Church, and the Dutch Reformed Church.

The congregational type.—It is probably true that the earliest Christian churches were independent of one another and had no organic system of fellowship. If this is true, the congregational form of church government is the oldest, though it was the latest to be fully developed.

The congregational theory.—This theory holds that a Christian church is one that is independent of any other in matters of control, though it associates and cooperates with other churches in Christian labors. The outstanding principle of congregationalism is the independence of each local congregation. Each local church elects its own officers, chooses and ordains its ministers, administers its discipline, and determines its mode of work without any form of external control. Each church is thus absolutely complete in itself, so that if all other churches should cease to be, it might become the mother church of another Christendom.

Congregational associations.—Congregationalism does not repudiate associations of churches, but advocates that they stand in the closest relation to one another in fellowship and assume obligations and duties that bind them into associations, which, however, must be voluntary. Hence, all the churches possessing this type of church government have voluntary conferences or associations or synods where problems that concern them are discussed, and recommendations made. The more important churches in the United States possessing this type of church government are the Congregational Church, the Baptist Church, the Disciples of Christ. Also, the Lutheran Church to a large extent belongs to this group, since the congregations retain the authority to call, elect, and ordain their own ministers.

Churches with a mixed form of government.—There is a large and important group of churches in the United States which have a mixed form of government. The largest and best known is the Methodist Episcopal Church, but there are others that have modeled their form of church polity after the Methodist Episcopal.

The Methodist Episcopal form.—Strictly speaking, the Methodist Episcopal form of church government is presbyterian, since it does not possess apostolic succession, which is the essential element in episcopal church government, and since it is ruled by elders. When John Wesley drew up the form of government for the American Methodist Church in 1784 he provided for general superintendents, who afterward took the name of bishops. These Methodist bishops, however, *are not a different order of the ministry, but are simply presbyters or elders elected to supervise.* Nor was it provided that the bishop should preside over a diocese, but he was to be a general superintendent. The Methodist bishop can exercise his authority anywhere.

The Methodist Conferences.—There are four chief kinds of Conferences in the Methodist Episcopal Church: the Quarterly Conference, made up of the pastor and the official members of the local church; the District Conference, composed of representatives from each church in the bounds of a district; the Annual Conference, made up of the pastors of the churches; and the General Conference, made up of an equal number of ministers and laymen representing Annual Conferences. The General Conference, which meets every four years, is the governing body of the church. It elects bishops, editors, general secretaries, and other general officials of the church, and also is the sole lawmaking body. It is presided over by the bishops, each in turn, but the bishops have no vote. According to Methodist usage and law the bishop is the sole authority in the appointment of pastors to the various churches, though the district superintendents act as an advisory body.

The Methodist system highly centralized.—The Methodist system of church government is perhaps the most highly centralized system in vogue in the United States, and the Methodist bishop has more power than any other Protestant church official. The bishop, however, is the servant of the General Conference and is held accountable to that body, which is of course a powerful check upon his authority.

Other churches having the Methodist Episcopal form of government.—Numerous churches have adopted with some modifications the Methodist system of church government. The Methodist Episcopal Church, South, differs somewhat in that the board of bishops is considered a coordinate body with the General Conference. The United Brethren Church, the Evangelical Churches, the African Methodist Episcopal, the African Methodist Episcopal Zion, and the Colored Methodist Episcopal Churches all have a form of government modeled after that of the original Methodist Episcopal Church.

QUESTIONS FOR DISCUSSION

1. What are the various types of church government?
2. What is the theory upon which papal church government rests and what is the scriptural basis for this theory?
3. Explain how the Roman Catholic Church is governed and give the names of the most important officials.

4. What is the episcopal theory of church government, and what is the principal element in this theory?

5. Explain how the episcopal system of church government functions. What are the most important Episcopal churches in the world?

6. Where and when did modern Presbyterianism arise?

7. Explain how the presbyterian form of church government is carried out in practice.

8. What is the congregational theory of the church? What are some of the congregational churches?

9. Discuss the Methodist Episcopal form of church government. In what respect is this form presbyterian? Why is it not episcopal in a strict sense?

10. Explain how the Methodist Episcopal type of church government functions. Name some of the churches which have this form of church government.

CHAPTER VI

THE BAPTISTS

BEFORE tracing the history of the Baptists in America it will be advantageous to understand clearly just what are the distinctive principles upon which the people known as Baptists stand. It has been generally supposed, among non-Baptists, that immersion was the primary and distinctive doctrine of this body of Christians. The name "Baptist" would signify this. The name, however, was not self-chosen. That group of people in the early Reformation period who insisted upon rebaptizing members who had been baptized in infancy were called in derision "Anabaptists," or "rebaptizers," or were sometimes called "Baptizers." This name was resented and earnestly repudiated, but as in other instances the name given in derision became fixed upon them and, instead of being a name of reproach, has become a name of honor.

Distinctive principles of Baptists.—Arranged in order of their importance the distinctive principles of the Baptists are: (1) the absolute supremacy of Scripture as a basis of faith and practice; (2) the opposition to infant baptism (Baptists maintain that not only is there no Scripture basis for infant baptism, but it is a perversion of an ordinance established by Christ); (3) the maintenance that every member must profess to be a personal partaker of salvation in Christ (infant baptism, they claim, is inconsistent with such a profession; for if infant baptism entitles a person to church membership, then necessarily many will become church members who are not regenerate members); (4) immersion (Baptists object to the prominent place given immersion by their opponents; but they insist, nevertheless, that immersion is the only form of baptism allowed by Scripture).

The Baptists and religious liberty.—From the beginning Baptists have been ardent champions of religious liberty, and here is their greatest contribution to the religious life of the world. Arising at a time when state and church were everywhere united, Baptists contended valiantly for the right of individuals to have complete religious liberty. They have always maintained that no human authority in church or state has any right to repress or hinder any man or group of men in the exercise of religious belief or worship. Baptists have always stood for the rights of the individual as against the close church organization. They have always accepted literally Luther's position of the universal priesthood of all believers and reject the conception of the ministry which would set aside any special group. They hold that Christ alone is their authority and their only Guide. Each church, as made up of the regenerate, "is competent to conduct its own affairs." As a self-governing spiritual democracy the church recognizes the spiritual freedom of each individual member. God speaks directly to men, and not to men through church authorities; therefore, the humblest believer is entitled to equal privileges in the church. Complete religious liberty implies the right to free association and organization, but any association of churches must be a voluntary and free association.

Baptists in the American colonies.—As we have already noticed, the Baptists were considered among the most radical religious groups in the American colonies. In at least eight of the colonies there were state churches, and in these colonies particularly Baptists were looked upon not only as religious radicals, but as enemies of all political and social order. Like the heretics of the Middle Ages they were thought of in many places about as we think of traitors to-day. Harsh treatment of Baptists, therefore, naturally followed, especially in Massachusetts, Connecticut, Virginia, and Maryland.

Origin of the American Baptists.—The American Baptists did not come historically from the English Baptists; rather, they date from the expulsion of Roger Williams from Massachusetts. Roger Williams, while a minister in the Congregational church at Salem, became a convert to Baptist views and as a result was relieved of his church and expelled from the colony. Leaving Massachusetts, he went to what is now Rhode Island, organized a colony, obtained a charter direct from the English Parliament in 1643, and invited all persecuted people to seek a refuge there. With this beginning Rhode Island became the chief Baptist center in the colonies. In the Quaker colonies of Pennsylvania, Delaware, and New Jersey, since there was a large degree of religious liberty there, Baptists were successful in establishing several churches. In New York and North Carolina a few scattered Baptist congregations were also formed. As late as 1740 there were only twenty-one Baptist churches in Massachusetts, Connecticut, and Rhode Island, the latter colony having eleven of that number.

The Great Awakening and its influence upon the Baptists.—The Baptists profited greatly from the Great Awakening that swept over the New England and middle colonies during the period from about 1735 to 1745. Throughout New England many Congregational churches were divided over the revival, and in numerous instances those who favored the evangelical methods separated from the conservatives and formed new churches. These New Light churches, as they were termed, were often deprived of rights by the more numerous Old Light churches. As a result many of them became out-and-out Baptist societies. So great was this movement in New England that by 1768 there were 12 Baptist churches in Connecticut, 30 in Massachusetts, and 36 in Rhode Island, making a total of 78, as contrasted with 21 in 1740. This growth continued until the Revolution not only in New England, but in the southern and middle colonies as well. In 1776 the Philadelphia Association had 29 churches. In 1784 Virginia had 151 churches, North Carolina 42, and South Carolina 27.

The Baptist Church on the early frontier.—Baptist principles of separation of church and state had triumphed in the American Revolution and were finally written into the Constitution. This fact gave the Baptists tremendous prestige at the very opening of the national period and accounts quite largely for their great ingatherings in the latter eighteenth and early nineteenth centuries. Especially were the Baptists popular on the frontier, where individualism was triumphant. It has been estimated that fully one fourth of the Baptists of Virginia emigrated to Kentucky and Tennessee between 1791 and 1810, and the Baptists were everywhere on the frontier both numerous and aggressive. This rapid growth has already been explained in a previous chapter.

The beginning of the missionary movement and its influence upon the Baptists.—The first missionary society among American Baptists was formed in 1814 and marks the beginning of a new era in the Baptist Church. Previously the Congregational, the Presbyterian, and the Reformed Churches had organized the American Board of Commissioners for Foreign Missions, and among the first missionaries sent out were Adoniram Judson and his wife, with Luther Rice. While on board ship bound for India they became convinced that immersion was the true method of baptism and on landing they immediately sent word to America of their conversion to Baptist views. It was as a result of this that the Baptist society was formed. Following the organization of the General Missionary Convention of the Baptist Denomination in the United States of America for Foreign Missions other Baptist societies were speedily formed. In 1824 a tract society was established, which developed into a publication society in 1840. In 1832 a home-missionary society was organized to care more adequately for the expanding work of the denomination in the new West. These denominational societies were responsible for bringing the various local churches into closer union and in creating a denominational consciousness that had hitherto been largely lacking.

The slavery schism in the Baptist Church.—The Baptist Church, being independent, or congregational, in its church government, was saved thereby from as serious a division as that which severed the Methodists. Like all other churches in the South the Baptists had identified themselves with the institution of slavery, while in the North, especially after 1830, abolition sentiment among Baptists greatly increased. Both Northern and Southern Baptists supported the Board of Foreign Missions, with headquarters in Boston, and it was inevitable that misunderstandings and differences should occur within the society over the question of slavery. The issue dividing the church finally arose over the matter of appointing slaveholders as missionaries. The Alabama State Baptist Convention raised the question in a series of resolutions in which it demanded that slaveholders share equally with nonslaveholders all the privileges and immunities of the several church societies, and stated "that they are entitled to receive any agency, mission, or other appointment which may run within the scope of their operations." In reply the missionary board frankly stated that it would never appoint a slaveholder as a missionary, nor would it be a party to any agreement that would imply approbation of slavery. This statement led to the withdrawal of the Southern conventions and to the organization of the Southern Baptist Convention. Since that time the Southern Baptists have remained a separate body. At present they are the largest white Baptist group in the United States, with a membership of 3,374,165.

Varieties of Baptists.—Besides the two great bodies of "regular" Baptists, already noted, the Colored Baptists deserve mention. With the close of the Civil War, Negro Baptist churches were numerously organized in the South, and to-day the Colored Baptist Church is the largest Baptist organization in the United States. The Free Will Baptists in the United States are divided into two groups, numbering together not more than one hundred thousand members. They reject the central doctrines of Calvinism and hold that salvation is equally possible to all. In church government they are presbyterian rather than congregational. The Primitive Baptists are those Baptists who object to denominational societies, such as missionary and tract societies. They hold to an extreme type of Calvinism, practice foot washing as well as immersion, and hold no conventions and have no schools. Even more extreme are the Two-Seed-in-the-Spirit Predestinarian Baptists. This type are usually antinomian; that is, they believe that God does not need nor does he want man's help in saving mankind, but that God will save men when and how he will.

The Dunkers and the Mennonites.—Two groups that may be classified as Baptists are the Dunkers, or Dunkards, or German Baptists; and the Mennonites, or Dutch Baptists. The Mennonites are named from Menno Simons, a native of Holland, who, as a priest in the Roman Catholic Church, began reading the Bible and in 1536 left that church to organize numerous societies for the purpose of worshiping as the Bible directed. With the opening of Pennsylvania to the persecuted of all kinds the Mennonites began to come to America, where they established their first church in Germantown. They have continued to come to America from Germany, Holland, and Switzerland, until now practically all the Mennonites in the world are to be found in the United States. Like the Mennonites the Dunkers began to come to Pennsylvania in the colonial period and to-day are found most numerously there. Both Mennonites and Dunkers are simple, earnest people, who try to follow the injunctions of the Bible literally. They are like the Quakers in some respects, as they are advocates of nonresistance. The Dunkers have a peculiar mode of immersion and also practice foot washing as a sacrament. The Mennonites do not as a rule immerse, but, rather, practice baptism by pouring. Both Dunkers and Mennonites have a type of presbyterian church government, and both are found most numerously in Pennsylvania, Ohio, Indiana, and Illinois.

Baptists and education.—For many years Brown University, founded in 1764, was the only Baptist institution conferring degrees; in more recent years, however, numerous colleges and universities have been founded by the Baptists, and some of them rank among the best institutions in the country. Such is true of the University of Chicago, the University of Rochester, Denison University, Colgate University, and Franklin College. At present there are more than a hundred universities and colleges and eleven theological seminaries under the control of the various Baptist groups.

Baptist leaders and preachers.—The intense individualism characteristic of the Baptists has created great leaders and preachers. Indeed, the spread of Baptist ideas and the remarkable growth of the denomination in the United States have been due to leadership rather than to organization. The Baptists have been particularly blessed with great preachers, such as Charles H. Spurgeon, the great English Baptist, who "preached to more people than any other man of the nineteenth century." In America to-day we have Russell H. Conwell, who was recently awarded a medal as the most useful citizen of the city of Philadelphia; William H. P. Faunce, president of Brown University; and Harry Emerson Fosdick, who to-day is perhaps the most influential preacher in America.

Baptist contributions to the religious life of America.— So great is the Baptist emphasis upon the individual and so little upon organization that it is correct to say that the Baptist denomination is not so much church as it is a movement under the impulse of a common experience. A Christian statesman recently summed up the contribution made by Baptists to the religious life of America as follows: Their first contribution is their intense loyalty to personal conviction. This loyalty is expressed in their practice of immersion. However we may differ from them as to the importance of this mode of baptism, we cannot but admire their loyalty to conviction in clinging to it. A second contribution is to be found in the simplicity of their creed. Their creed is the Bible, and they have consistently refused to make any authoritative statement of their beliefs, such as is found in the Twenty-five Articles of the Methodists or in the Westminster Confession of the Presbyterians. A third contribution is their strong insistence upon the entire separation of church and state. We have come to think of this as a matter of course, as one of those things which go without saying; but it was not always so nor is it so to-day in many lands. Roger Williams' insistence upon the separation of church and state led to his banishment from Massachusetts, and from that day until now Baptists have led the way in the battles for religious and civil liberty. They have ever been ready to go all lengths in their insistence upon the entire separation of church and state. That verse of Scripture which best sums up the position of the Baptists is: "Stand fast therefore, and be not entangled again in a yoke of bondage." The Baptists would say, "Let every man be true—true to the voice within, true to his personal convictions of right and wrong, true to the American spirit of separation of church and state, true to God—that he may enter into the full inheritance that belongs to every child of the Most High." "The Baptist Church is a glorious church, for she bore and still bears testimony to the primitive mode of baptism, to the purity of the congregation, to the separation of church and state, and the liberty of conscience."

QUESTIONS FOR DISCUSSION

1. How did the Baptists get their name?

2. What are the distinctive principles of Baptists? What is their historic attitude toward religious liberty?

3. How were Baptists considered in the colonial period and why? Describe the career of Roger Williams.

4. In what way did the Great Awakening increase the number of Baptists in the colonies?

5. What were the reasons which account for the popularity of the Baptists on the frontier?

6. How did the missionary movement effect the Baptists? Who were their first foreign missionaries, and when was their missionary society organized?

7. Explain how the question of slavery divided the Baptist Church.

8. What are the chief divisions of the Baptists to-day, and in what way do they differ from one another?

9. What has been some of the outstanding contributions of the Baptists to religious life in America?

10. Who have been some of the great Baptist preachers and leaders in America?

CHAPTER VII

THE ROMAN CATHOLICS

THE official name of the church popularly known as the Catholic is the Holy Catholic Apostolic Roman Church. It includes that part of the Christian church which recognizes the Bishop of Rome, or the Pope, as the head of the church and dates its origin from the apostle Peter.

Differences between Catholicism and Protestantism.—A primary difference between Catholics and Protestants lies in their different attitude toward the Bible. The Catholics teach that the Bible does not contain all the truth that Christ revealed, while the Protestants hold that the Bible contains all the essential teachings of Christ. The Protestant view is well summed up in Article V of the Articles of Religion of the Methodist Episcopal Church, which states: "The Holy Scriptures contains all things necessary to salvation; so that whatsoever is not read therein, nor may be proved thereby, is not to be required of any man that it should be believed as an article of faith, or be thought requisite or necessary to salvation." On the other hand, Catholics contend that "the truths Christ revealed are contained partially in the Bible, partially in ecclesiastical tradition." They further hold that the Catholic Church is independent of the Bible, existed before the Bible, and would continue to exist unchanged without the Bible. Thus, they practically admit that many of their practices and doctrines may not necessarily have a strong scriptural basis, nor do they need such a basis, since the church is held to be, in a sense, above the Bible, and alone competent to interpret the Bible.

The Pope the vicar of Christ on earth.—The Catholic Church, so all Catholics believe, was founded by the apostles in the first century and has been governed by the lineal descendants of the apostles since that time. Its doctrines have never changed and are unchangeable. The

Pope, since he is Christ's representative on earth, when he speaks in that capacity "in matters of faith and morals" is of equal authority with the Bible and is infallible. Catholics are taught that as all Protestant churches were founded by human beings, while their own church is the only one founded by Christ, their church is the one and only true church. Therefore, to be saved, membership in this true church is necessary.

Important Roman Catholic doctrines.—The Roman Catholic Church teaches that Christ instituted seven sacraments. These are baptism, confirmation, penance, the holy Eucharist, or the Lord's Supper; extreme unction, holy orders, or ordination; and matrimony. On the other hand, the Protestant churches maintain that Christ instituted only two sacraments—baptism and the Lord's Supper. The Catholics teach that baptism is absolutely necessary for salvation, for in that way, and in that way only, can original sin be washed away. They hold that Christ is "really, truly, and substantially present" in the bread and wine of the sacrament of the Lord's Supper, or the sacrifice of the mass, as they call it, and that this sacrifice is the same as the sacrifice of Christ on the cross. They maintain that Christ ordained priests at the Last Supper the night before he died, and "that the true religion of Christ is impossible without a priest, an altar, and a sacrifice." Further, Catholics are taught that Christ gave priests the power to forgive sins, and that our sins can be forgiven only through the priest. They teach the existence of purgatory, an intermediate state between heaven and this world, and therefore, they believe that prayers for the dead ought to be made. They venerate relics of Christ and the saints and teach that statues and pictures of Christ and the saints are worthy of veneration.

First Roman Catholic churches in America.—The Spaniards established the first permanent colonies in what is now the United States; therefore, the first missionaries in this territory were Catholics. In most of the expeditions conducted in the early fifteen hundreds by the Spaniards, in and around the Gulf of Mexico, Spanish priests were present. These priests not only conducted worship for the members of the expeditions, but made feeble attempts to

Christianize the Indians with whom they came in contact. Thus, Coronado's expedition into New Mexico (1540) contained Spanish priests who preached to the Indians, and the Spaniards established a church in Saint Augustine, Florida, as early as 1565. The Spaniards were busy founding missions on the Pacific Coast, in what is now California, in the seventeenth and eighteenth centuries; and on the Atlantic Coast, in what is now Maine and about the Great Lakes, French Catholic priests were founding missions among the Indians. Attempts also were made to make converts of the Iroquois tribes in what is now the State of New York.

Catholics in England.—As we have already seen, England had become definitely Protestant in the reign of Queen Elizabeth, and severe laws were passed against the Catholics because of their constant plottings to overthrow the queen. As a result of these laws there were very few among the common people of England who remained in the Catholic Church, though many among the nobility and the large landowners did not give up their attachment for the old church. Ireland, however, was still largely Catholic and was to remain so even though both Elizabeth and King James I attempted to temper Irish Catholicism with Scotch Presbyterian colonists, and north Ireland became predominately Protestant. Since there were so few Catholics in England during the colonizing period, very few came out to America, the largest number coming to Maryland, the colony of the Catholic nobleman, Lord Baltimore.

The Catholic colony of Maryland.—Previously to his profession of Catholicism, Lord Baltimore had been secretary of state under King James I; but when he announced himself a Catholic in 1625 he resigned that post and devoted himself to the project of establishing a colony for Catholics in America. He received a charter for a large tract of land in America (1632), to which he gave the name "Maryland," in honor of the queen. In 1633 twenty gentlemen and some two hundred laborers were sent out to Maryland. The twenty gentlemen were Catholics, but most of the laborers were Protestants, and it is probable that even from the beginning the Protestants outnumbered

THE ROMAN CATHOLICS

the Catholics in Baltimore's colony. It was thought and hoped by the founders of Maryland that English Catholics, because of the laws against their faith, would gladly seek a refuge in America; but the migration of English Catholics failed to materialize, and when it was seen that Catholics were refusing to come to the colony, the proprietors became more willing to receive settlers of other faiths. Lord Baltimore was undoubtedly a true Catholic, but he was likewise a tolerant and public-spirited man. Accordingly, he sent word to New England in 1643 that all creeds would be protected in Maryland and likewise took steps to restrain the activities of the Jesuits, who were getting a firm hold in the colony.

Catholics outnumbered and disfranchised.—These measures of Lord Baltimore soon brought into Maryland numerous groups of Protestants, among them being a group of more than a thousand Puritans, who came from Virginia to escape the despotism of Governor Berkeley. It was not long until the more numerous Protestants gained control of the government and, instead of granting toleration to Catholics, proceeded to disfranchise them. Public worship by Catholics was forbidden by law.

Catholic restrictions in other colonies.—There were a few Catholics in the other colonies, particularly in Pennsylvania and New York. One of the better-known colonial governors—Governor Dongan of the latter colony—was of that faith. In the eighteenth century a few Catholics emigrated from Ireland, but the number throughout the colonial period was never large nor influential. Everywhere they were regarded with suspicion by their Protestant neighbors and they were under legal disabilities of one kind or another everywhere. As a whole the Roman Catholics had little influence in the colonial period and little to do with establishing American independence and in the formation of American institutions. However, John Carroll, of Maryland, a Catholic, signed the Declaration of Independence; and the sixth article of the Constitution, abolishing religious tests as a qualification for any public office, was adopted largely through the influence of a memorial presented to the convention by Carroll.

The Catholic Church following the Revolution.—Soon

after the close of the Revolution, the Rev. John Carroll, of Maryland, was consecrated a bishop, with headquarters at Baltimore. At that time it is estimated that there were about 30,000 Catholics in the United States, Maryland having about 16,000 of that number, and Pennsylvania 7,000. There were several old French posts in what is now Illinois, Indiana, and Michigan, where several thousand French-speaking Catholics were to be found. Soon after independence the Catholics made a beginning in Kentucky and Ohio, but the great increase in the American Catholic Church did not begin until immigration set in from Ireland and other Catholic countries of Europe. By 1807 it has been estimated that the Catholic population of the United States numbered about 150,000.

The Catholic Church increased by immigration.—The Roman Catholic Church in the United States has grown rapidly, especially since 1820. This increase has been due almost entirely to immigration from Roman Catholic Ireland, from Germany, and, more recently, from Italy and other Southern European countries where Roman Catholicism predominates. The great migration from Ireland to America began about 1820, was greatly augmented by the terrible potato-rot famine of 1845–46, and since that time has been a steady stream. This tremendous influx of Catholic Irish into the United States soon made the Irish the predominating element in the Catholic Church in America, and this Irish control has been largely maintained. A conception of the vastness of the Irish immigration may be obtained when it is considered that about 1820 Ireland had, in round numbers, a population of eight million, while to-day Ireland's population is not more than half that number.

German Catholic migration.—Beginning in 1830, due to revolutionary movements in southern Germany, a great stream of Germans began to come to America. They came largely from that part of Germany where the Roman Catholics are strongest. The revolution of 1848 augmented this German migration, which continued steadily until the unification of the German Empire about 1860. This German population went largely into the Central West—into Missouri and Wisconsin. Cities such as Cincinnati, Saint Louis, Chicago, and Milwaukee received a large German Catholic increase in population.

Italian and Southern European Catholic immigration.— Within recent years the largest increase in the Catholic population of the United States has come from Italy and other Southern European countries. This population has gone into the larger cities of the Eastern States—Boston, New York City, and Philadelphia—though many have made their way into the cities and towns of the Middle West, and nearly every good-sized town in the country now possesses a few Italian Roman Catholics. Besides these larger groups of European Catholics there are numerous Polish Catholics, and others especially from Southeastern Europe. Meanwhile there has been a considerable migration of French-speaking Catholics from lower Canada, who have come largely into the mill towns of New England.

Increase of American Catholics since 1820.—It has been estimated that by 1830 there were 600,000 Catholics in the United States. This number by 1850 had grown to 3,500,000. At the outbreak of the Civil War the Catholic population had increased another million. In 1876 it had reached 6,500,000. Statistics for 1922 give the Catholic membership in the United States at 18,104,804.

American Catholic bishops and archbishops.—Baltimore was the head of the first Catholic diocese, established in 1789. New Orleans became the head of the second in 1793. In 1808 Baltimore was made the seat of an archdiocese, and in the same year Boston, New York City, and Philadelphia became the seats of bishops. Gradually most of the large cities in the United States have become the seats of bishops or archbishops. At present there are seventeen archbishops and eighty-five bishops in the United States. The number of priests ministering to congregation is 22,049.

Catholic education in the United States.—From the beginning Catholics have maintained parochial schools for the education of Catholic children. They have been more or less critical of the public-school system, often accusing it of ungodliness and irreligion. This attitude has furnished ground for suspicion of the Catholic Church, on the part of non-Catholics, which is not altogether undeserved. In 1920 there were 1,795,673 Catholic children in parochial schools in the United States, under 54,265 teachers. Besides the parochial schools the Catholics maintain 1,552 high schools and numerous colleges and universities. Among the better-known Catholic universities are the Catholic University of America at Washington, Notre Dame in Indiana, Fordham in New York, and Marquette University in Milwaukee.

Roman Catholic contributions to the religious life of America.—The Roman Catholic Church is a vast, world-wide institution, with a history that goes far back, even beyond the beginnings of our modern civilization. It would be very hard to account for that long life if it had not made great contributions to society. In summing up the contributions made by the Catholic Church to the life of America, I can do no better than take some of Dean Brown's suggestions: *First,* the Roman Catholics have inculcated the habit of worship into their own people. This is an example that Protestant people everywhere might well follow. Catholics go to church to worship, never to be merely entertained or to hear a sermon. One cannot go into a Catholic church, whether on Sunday or during the week, without feeling the very atmosphere of worship all about him. *Secondly,* the Catholic Church represents authority, and its people have the habit of obedience. We as Protestants cannot recognize an infallible Pope and we are all agreed in opposing the claims of the Catholic Church to temporal authority; but at the same time we can be grateful for the great moral influence exercised by the Catholic Church over millions of people. The great immigrant hordes that have been pouring into the United States for more than a hundred years would have been a much more serious menace but for the control exercised over the majority of them by the Catholic Church. We may not agree on all the teachings of the Catholic Church in regard to morality, but their opposition to the terrible divorce evil and the way they have set themselves against "the revolutionary type of social agitation" has undoubtedly been of great service to American life. *Thirdly,* the Roman Catholic Church has contributed richly toward the "promotion of the spirit of trust in the unseen." Catholic worship is largely symbolical. The seven sacraments, providing some measure of spiritual direction for every age and every crisis of life, continually suggest to the faithful Catholic the reality of the unseen. Americans are very practical people—people inclined to believe in those things only which can be seen and handled. We are prone to think that money can buy all the help available, and it is well to have among us a church that continually holds up before us "those intangible aids which mean so much in the gaining of that more abundant life to which we are all called." *Fourthly,* in the establishment of hospitals and charities the Catholic Church has led the way in America, and American Protestantism is only just beginning to undertake its share of this work. Through all the years the Catholic Church can point to innumerable of her faithful children who have ever been willing to render sacrificial service to mankind.

Distrust of Catholics.—There has always been a feeling of distrust of Roman Catholics on the part of many Protestants. This has come down to us from the colonial period and from our Old World ancestors. The distrust is due not alone to the religious teachings of the Catholic Church, but, rather, to the dread of political control by the Catholic population. This fear has led to the formation of numerous anti-Catholic parties in the course of our history. Such were the Know Nothing, or Native American Party of the fifties, the A. P. A., or the American Protective Association of a generation ago, and the present Ku Klux Klan. Such organizations have roused antagonism and hatred and, instead of solving a difficult problem, they have only added to its difficulty. Is not the cultivation of a mutual spirit of appreciation and understanding between American Protestants and Catholics far more effective and certainly more Christian in helping to solve the difficult problem of living together happily and as Christians?

QUESTIONS FOR DISCUSSION

1. What is the Roman Catholic attitude toward the Bible as contrasted with the Protestant position?

2. What are some of the most important doctrines of the Roman Catholic Church?

3. Where and when did the Spanish and French establish the first Catholic churches in America?

4. What was the position of Roman Catholics in England in the seventeenth century? Why were there so few Catholics in America during the colonial period?

5. Describe the founding of Maryland by Lord Baltimore. What motives led Lord Baltimore to open his colony to all, Catholics and Protestants alike?

6. How were Catholics treated in the colonies generally? How numerous were the Catholics in America at the close of the Revolution?

7. What effect has immigration had upon the increase of the Catholic population in the United States? From what countries in Europe have the Catholics chiefly come?

8. What is the Catholic position on the question of the public schools? Why do they maintain parochial schools?

9. What have been some of the chief contributions made by the Catholics to the religious life of America?

10. Why have Protestant people distrusted Catholics? What in your opinion is the best way to solve the problem of Catholics and Protestants living together?

CHAPTER VIII

THE CONGREGATIONALISTS AND THE EPISCO-PALIANS

THE two most important churches throughout the colonial period were the Congregationalists of New England and the Anglicans, or, as we call them to-day, the Episcopalians. The Congregational was the state church in Massachusetts and Connecticut. The Anglican was the established church in the Southern colonies.

What is Congregationalism?—Broadly speaking, any church in which the congregation is independent of other congregations, and which frames its own statement of doctrine, selects its own minister and ordains him, and elects all its own officials is a congregational church. Thus, the Baptist, the Lutheran, and the Disciple Churches are congregational so far as their church government is concerned. But, strictly speaking, there is only one Congregational denomination—that which had its beginnings in New England at the founding of Plymouth in 1620. Calvinism was predominant among New England Congregationalists at the beginning, but the modern view, at least, would not bar others from their churches.

The beginning of American Congregationalism.—Congregationalism began in America with the landing of the Pilgrims at Plymouth in 1620. They were already organized as a congregation before coming to America, having separated from the English Church before leaving England, and their ten years' residence in Holland had welded them into a self-sufficient body. When, a few years later, the Massachusetts Bay Colony was established (1628) by a group of Puritan Church of England men, the great distance from England soon caused them to sever their relationship with the Established Church, and they adopted the form of church government already in vogue at Plymouth. Within the next ten years (1628–38) two other

Congregational colonies were formed—Connecticut in 1634 and New Haven in 1638.

The Puritan migration to America.—The years from 1620 to 1640 were in England a period of Puritan persecution due to the policy adopted by James I and Charles I of compelling uniformity of worship. As a result of this policy of the English government from twenty to forty thousand English Puritans came out to America during these twenty years. Many of the English Puritans had been in the Church of England but on coming to America they adopted Congregational views. In 1640 every church in New England but two was Congregational.

Church and state.—In Massachusetts and Connecticut it was considered the duty of the state to support the church, and the inhabitants, whether church members or not, were taxed to support the Congregational ministers. In 1631 Massachusetts passed a resolution stating "that no man shall be admitted to the freedom of the body politic but such as are members of some of the churches within the limits of the same." Of course, in this close association of church and state Massachusetts and Connecticut were simply following Old World precedents. Gradually, however, a measure of toleration was allowed to other churches, and by 1800 there were 151 other churches in Massachusetts besides the Congregational.

The founding of Harvard and Yale.—Perhaps the most important influence of Congregationalism in America in the three hundred years of its history has been exerted through its educational institutions. Its first colleges were established primarily to provide training for its ministers. Thus in 1636 Harvard College was established at Cambridge, the General Court of Massachusetts voting four hundred pounds for that purpose. Later, in 1701, Yale was founded by the more conservative members of the church because they deplored the liberal tendencies of Harvard. Following the establishment of these two original Congregational colleges others were founded until now they are to be found from the Atlantic to the Pacific. No group of colleges and universities in America has exerted a finer influence upon American education. Of the older Congregational colleges, besides Harvard and Yale, the following are the best known: Williams College, founded in 1791; Dartmouth, founded in 1770; Bowdoin, founded in 1794; and the University of Vermont, 1800. A later group of Congregational colleges is represented by Western Reserve University, Oberlin College, Beloit College, Knox College, Grinnell College, and Carlton College.

Early Congregational leaders.—The Congregationalists have among their list of leaders some of the greatest names in American history. Jonathan Edwards has been called the greatest man produced in the colonial period. Certainly he was the greatest preacher and theologian of that period. His part in the Great Awakening and in education in the latter eighteenth century was conspicuous. Following Edwards were Samuel Hopkins (1721–1803), Joseph Bellamy (1719–90), and Timothy Dwight—men responsible for the revival of Congregationalism in the years following the Revolution. The greatest of all the Protestant missionaries to the Indians in the colonial period was John Eliot, a Congregational minister.

Congregational missionaries in the West.—Soon after the Revolution people from New England began to move beyond the Allegheny Mountains and form new settlements along the Ohio. Marietta was the first New England settlement in the West and was founded in 1788. A few years later people from Connecticut began to fill up the Western Reserve in northeastern Ohio, and in these settlements Congregational churches were planted. Hand in hand with the planting of Congregational settlements and churches came the Congregational college. In 1801 a plan of union with the Presbyterian Church was arranged whereby Congregationalists going West generally joined Presbyterian churches. This plan stopped the growth of Congregationalism in the West until after the abrogation of the plan in 1852. Since that time there has been some growth of Congregationalism in the Central Western States, especially in Illinois and in some of the Northwestern States. Congregationalists had little chance to grow in the South before the Civil War because of their strong opposition to slavery.

The Unitarian split.—The most serious split in the Congregational Church occurred during the opening years of the nineteenth century. This was the Unitarian movement, largely fathered by William Ellery Channing, a great Boston preacher. The Unitarian movement was a reaction against the stern Calvinism aroused by the Great Awakening. By the opening of the nineteenth century many Congregational churches in New England were split over the question of the Trinity, and it was not long before Harvard College came under the control of the Unitarians. In many instances the Unitarians were numerous enough to retain the old church building, the orthodox remainder of the congregation withdrawing and building a new church. Thus, many New England churches were divided, and by 1815 the Unitarians were recognized as a distinct denomination.

The pioneering work of the Congregationalists.—The Congregationalists have exercised an influence much greater than their numbers would indicate. Not only were the first American colleges founded by them, but numerous other movements had their beginnings among them, such as foreign missions, theological seminaries for the special training of ministers, missionary work among the Indians, and special work for the Negroes in the South. The Congregationalists likewise led the way in higher education for women, Mount Holyoke College, a Congregational institution for women, being the first of the kind in the United States. No church has had a greater group of preachers than the Congregational. Among the most noted are Horace Bushnell, Lyman Beecher, Henry Ward Beecher, and, at the present time, S. Parkes Cadman and Charles E. Jefferson.

Congregational statistics to-day.—Statistics for 1922 credit the Congregational Church in the United States with a membership of 838,271, with 5,873 churches and 5,781 ministers. Under their control are forty-three colleges and universities, and they maintain ten theological seminaries.

The contribution of the Congregationalists.—No church has had a finer influence upon American society than the Congregationalist. It was the Congregational Church that introduced pure democracy in America. Other churches have come to adopt this form of church government, but the Congregationalist churches were the first to practice it. Perhaps the greatest contribution of the Congregationalists has come through their emphasis upon education. They have founded more colleges, in proportion to their numbers, than any other church in America—fifty-six. From the beginning theirs has been a teaching church and it has produced a long and noble list of educators—Jonathan Edwards, Mark Hopkins, Timothy Dwight, Austin Phelps, Edward Park, Charles G. Finney; Mary Lyon, of Mount Holyoke; Alice Freeman Palmer, of Wellesley; and, in more recent years, Daniel G. Gilman, of Johns Hopkins; Cyrus Northrup, of the University of Minnesota; and James B. Angell, of Michigan. It has likewise made a distinct contribution in its great preachers. The Congregationalists have been the trail breakers in many a new undertaking. The first missionaries to the Indians were theirs, they formed the first American foreign-missionary society, the first group of foreign missionaries came from a Congregational college, they were the first to undertake the education of freedmen after the Civil War, and they led the way in the translation of the Scriptures into foreign languages for missionary work. It would indeed be difficult to find anywhere a group of people of equal size who have exercised a greater influence for good in the world than the people whom we call Congregationalists.

The Episcopalians.—We have already noticed the fact that the Anglican, or Established Church of England was one of the two most important colonial churches, and we have traced the part it played up to the close of the American Revolution. It is now our purpose to follow the growth of the Protestant Episcopal Church from the close of the Revolution to the present.

The Anglican Church at the close of the Revolution.—At the close of the American Revolution many of the Anglican churches in the United States were without ministers, for a large number of their clergymen went back to England at the outbreak of the war. In 1775 there had been 164 Anglican churches and chapels in Virginia, with 91 clergymen; but at the close of the war only 28 clergymen remained, and 95 of the parishes were either extinct or forsaken. In New England only two Anglican churches had been kept open during the war. A large majority of the laymen, however, had been patriots, and it is significant that two thirds of the signers of the Declaration of Independence were Episcopalians. At the close of the Revolution there was naturally a strong prejudice against anything that savored of England, and the Episcopalians were too nearly allied to the Established Church of England to gain popular approval. As a result of this attitude it was many years before they were able to show a gain.

The organization of the Protestant Episcopal Church.— With independence a group of Anglican clergymen and laymen from New York, New Jersey, and Pennsylvania met at New Brunswick, New Jersey, in May, 1784, and there passed resolutions looking toward the formation of a new national church entirely independent of the old English Church. In the fall of the same year another group, from Delaware and Maryland, together with those from the Middle States, called a general convention to meet in September, 1785, in Philadelphia, to draw up a constitution, prepare a liturgy, and take such steps as were necessary to secure the consecration of a bishop for America. This program was successfully carried through, and by 1787 three bishops had been elected and consecrated—Bishop Seabury for Connecticut, Bishop White for New York, and Bishop Provoost for Pennsylvania. A little later Bishop James Madison was selected for Virginia. The constitution of the new church provided that "the Protestant Episcopal Church be independent of all foreign authority; that it have full and exclusive power to regulate the concerns of its own communion; that the doctrines be maintained as in the Church of England; that bishops, priests, and deacons be required; and that the canons and laws be made by a more representative body of clergymen and laity conjointly."

Slow development during the early years.—The Protestant Episcopal Church had little chance to grow during the early years of our national history. It was a period of emotionalism in religion, and the service of the Episcopal church was considered formal. Moreover, the church was still regarded by many people as under English influence if not under English control. At the first general convocation, held in 1792, there were not more than two hundred clergymen in the country. By 1832 the number of clergymen had increased to six hundred, and the church was beginning to gain a foothold in the newer sections of the nation.

Pioneer work in the West.—By 1812 a new zeal and devotion seems to have appeared, and a group of energetic bishops were consecrated to take the direction of the work, especially in the newer States. Among these new and able bishops were John Henry Hobart, who became bishop of New York; Richard C. Moore, of Virginia, whose interest in education resulted in the founding of two seminaries for the training of ministers—one in New York in 1819, and the other in Alexandria, Virginia, in 1824. Pioneer work in Ohio, Indiana, and Illinois was begun under the direction of Bishop Philander Chase, one of the ablest and most devoted of men. This great leader was responsible for the founding of Kenyon College in Ohio in 1824. Between 1835 and the opening of the Civil War the work of founding new dioceses continued, and the church was established in Iowa and other Central Western States and in the new sections of the South, as well as in California and Oregon. By 1850 there were 1,558 Episcopal clergymen in the United States, with about 80,000 members. At the close of the Civil War the membership had grown to 150,000.

Effect of the Civil War upon the Episcopal Church.—With the secession of the Confederate States and the opening of the Civil War the Episcopal Church in the South organized the "Protestant Episcopal Church in the Confederate States." The church in the North, however, refused to recognize the withdrawal of the Southern churches, and at the general convention held in 1862 the roll of the Southern dioceses was called. This attitude probably prevented a more serious split, for at the end of the war the Southern dioceses resumed their accustomed place in the general convention without any serious consequences.

Since the Civil War.—The growth of the Episcopal Church since the Civil War has been large though not phenomenal, keeping pace with the expansion and growth of the nation. The latest statistics give ninety dioceses and missionary districts in the United States and eleven missionary districts abroad. The Episcopal Church has had its largest success in the cities, where beautiful and imposing churches and cathedrals have been erected. The membership numbers 1,118,396, with 8,324 churches and 6,024 ministers. The Episcopalians have only a small number of colleges under their control, the best known being the University of the South, Trinity College in Hartford, Connecticut, and Kenyon College in Ohio. They maintain, however, fourteen theological seminaries for the training of ministers.

How the Episcopal Church is governed.—The Episcopal Church is a church ruled by bishops. At the head of each diocese is a bishop elected by a diocesan convention made up of lay and clerical members. The duties of bishops are to ordain ministers, or priests, assist in the consecration of other bishops, preside over the diocesan convention, institute ministers, or rectors of parishes, confirm members, and visit each church at least once every three years. Every three years the General Convention, the lawmaking body of the church, meets. This is made up of two houses—the house of bishops and the house of clerical and lay delegates.

The doctrinal position of the Episcopal Church.—The Episcopal Church accepts all the historic creeds and holds to the Thirty-nine Articles of Religion of the Established Church of England. It has three orders of the clergy—deacons, priests, and bishops. Perhaps its outstanding feature is its position on the historic episcopacy and the doctrine of apostolic succession. The tendency in recent years, among the clergymen particularly, is toward high-churchism. There have been numerous attempts to change the name of the church to the American Catholic Church, as the high-church group repudiates Protestantism and holds that the church is not a Protestant church. This attempt, however, has always failed, due largely to the opposition of the laymen in the house of deputies.

Contributions of the Protestant Episcopal Church.—The Protestant Episcopal occupies a peculiar place among the churches in the United States. Because of its historic connection with the Established Church of England and the important place it occupied in the colonial period, together with its historic and dignified ritual, its influence has been much greater than its numbers would indicate. The Episcopal Church has contributed to the religious life of America a dignified and beautiful form of worship. As a rule, Episcopal churches are always churchly, whether large or small. And all this is emphasized not for mere beauty's sake but as an aid to worship. Such surroundings do greatly influence us, and whenever we may enter an Episcopal church we shall find there "an atmosphere of worship, of aspiration, of yearning for fellowship with the unseen." Again, the Episcopal Church has kept a vital connection with all that is good, inspiring, and beautiful in the past. It traces its connection back to the apostles; and its *Book of Common Prayer,* to which we are all debtors, contains all the ancient forms of worship which have been developed through the Christian centuries. In a new country such as ours, with its great variety of churches and forms of worship, we need just such an influence among us as that exerted by the Protestant Episcopal Church, with its historic and dignified liturgy.

QUESTIONS FOR DISCUSSION

1. What is congregationalism in its broadest sense? What is Congregationalism in the denominational sense? When and where did American Congregationalism begin?

2. What has been the educational influence of the Congregationalists in the United States? What are some of their most famous institutions of learning?

3. In what movements have the Congregationalists done pioneer work? Who have been some of their great preachers and educators?

4. Why was the Protestant Episcopal Church slow in developing following the American Revolution?

5. Compare the Congregational and the Episcopal Churches in numbers and in the nature of their influence in America.

6. What has been the peculiar contributions made by the Episcopalians to the religious life of America?

CHAPTER IX

THE LUTHERANS

THE Lutherans are those Christians who profess to follow most closely the teachings of the great German reformer, Martin Luther. They accept the great historic creeds of Christendom and hold to the Augsburg Confession, which was adopted by the Diet of Augsburg, June 25, 1530. In this confession the doctrine of justification by faith alone is central and is set forth clearly and briefly in a section by itself. The Lutherans accept the two ordinances of baptism and the Lord's Supper, though the Lutheran view of the Lord's Supper is peculiar to them. They hold that "in the Holy Supper there are present with the elements and are received sacramentally and supernaturally the body and blood of the Lord Jesus Christ." This supernatural presence of Christ in the sacrament does not require, however, any special priestly miracle, as is taught by the Roman Catholics. The Lutherans have a formal and liturgical form of service and are accustomed to observe the festivals of the Christian year more strictly than do most Protestant churches.

The Lutheran type of church government.—The Lutheran Church in the United States is basically congregational in its form of church government. The congregation calls its pastor, though he is usually ordained by the synod, and the internal affairs of each church are administered by a church council and the pastor. The synod is composed of the pastors of the several congregations and elected lay delegates from the churches of a certain district. The synods in turn send delegates to the general synod.

Lutheran bodies in America.—Altogether there are twenty distinct Lutheran Churches in the United States, the most important being the United Lutheran Church in America, which was recently organized as the result of the uniting of the three older Lutheran bodies—the General Synod, the General Council, and the United Synod of the South. The more important other Lutheran bodies are the Joint Synod of Ohio; the Iowa Synod; the Augustana Synod, which is the Swedish branch of the Lutheran Church; the Norwegian Lutheran Church; two Danish Lutheran Churches; two Finnish Churches; an Icelandic Synod; the Missouri Synod; and the Wisconsin Synod. All these bodies are similar in doctrine and organization, and many of them are separate because of racial and language differences and peculiarities developed in various Lutheran state churches in Europe.

The coming of the first Lutherans to America.—The first Lutheran congregations in America were in the Dutch colony of New Amsterdam and among the Swedes on the Delaware. There seem to have been a few Lutherans among the Dutch colonists at New Amsterdam from the first, where they enjoyed some degree of religious freedom, though the Reformed Church of Holland was the state church in the colony. There came to be, by about the middle of the seventeenth century, two Dutch Lutheran congregations: one at Albany and the other at New Amsterdam; but under the rule of Governor Stuyvesant they were treated harshly. In 1656 the governor forbade even private worship in the homes of the Lutherans; and the next year, when the first Lutheran pastor arrived in the person of John Ernst Goetwater, he was not allowed to remain. Relief did not come to the Dutch Lutherans in America until the English captured the Dutch colony in 1664, when they were allowed complete liberty of worship.

Early Lutherans among the Swedes.—The Swedes organized a company in 1626 for the purpose of planting a colony in America. It was not until 1638, however, that two vessels brought out the first Swedish colonists to the Delaware, where they founded Christina on the site where Wilmington, Delaware, now stands. Lutheranism had become the state church of Sweden, and very naturally the Lutheran Church was established in this first Swedish colony in America. The first Swedish Lutheran pastor came out in 1639, and Swedish churches were built in Philadelphia in 1700 and in Christina (Wilmington) in 1697. The Swedes were in what is now southeast Philadelphia as early as 1639 and prepared the way with the Indians for the coming of William Penn. The Swedish colony on the Delaware, however, was short-lived, for in 1655 Governor Stuyvesant of New Amsterdam captured it, though one of the terms of capitulation was that the Lutherans were to enjoy freedom of worship and were to be allowed a Lutheran minister. After the death of their first pastor John Campanius was sent over, who was not only occupied with the congregation at Christina but was also active in missionary work among the Indians and made a translation of Luther's *Smaller Catechism* in the Delaware tongue some years before John Eliot began his translation of the Bible for Indian use. By the end of the century, thanks to the effective work of several devoted pastors sent out from Sweden and Holland, the Swedes had several congregations in the vicinity of their first colony.

The coming of Lutherans from Germany.—Of much greater importance, from the standpoint of the founding of Lutheranism in America, than the early Dutch and Swedish Lutherans was the coming of German immigrants to Pennsylvania. When William Penn established his great colony of Pennsylvania he welcomed all persecuted Protestants, and among those who gladly accepted his invitation were the Germans. Indeed, William Penn made two visits to Germany in the interests of his colony, and on the opening of his colony an invitation was sent to the Germans in their own tongue. Germantown, Pennsylvania, laid out in 1685, is a testimony to the fact that the Germans came early to Penn's great colony. The first Germans to come, however, were German Quakers and Mennonites rather than Lutherans.

The Palatinate German migration.—The great migration from southern Germany began in the years 1708 to 1709 and was brought about by peculiar conditions prevailing in Europe. Louis XIV of France began a series of wars to push the French boundary to the Rhine, and the Germans living in what is known as the Palatinate region of the Rhine suffered greatly because of these French invasions. There were also religious reasons for discontent, as the state religion in the various small German states was determined by each petty prince and sometimes without regard to the wishes of his subjects. As a result of this situation harsh treatment was meted out especially to members of mystic and pietistic German sects. The migration, which began in 1708 and 1709, continued with little interruption until past the middle of the century. It has been estimated that between 1727 and 1754 there was an annual average of two thousand German immigrants coming to America. Some of these immigrants settled in New York, New Jersey, Maryland, Virginia, and Georgia; but the largest proportion of them came to Pennsylvania, and at the outbreak of the Revolution it is thought that they made up about one third of the total population of Pennsylvania.

The German Lutherans in America.—The German Lutherans who came out in this great migration were at first largely without pastors, and appeals were made to the Swedish Lutheran pastors on the Delaware to help them. The appeal did not go unheeded, but the help the Swedish pastors could render by no means satisfied the great need. Finally, an appeal was sent to Germany. After much delay Henry Melchior Mühlenberg was sent out to take charge of the German Lutherans in America. The coming of Mühlenberg in 1742 was one of the most important events in the history of the American Lutheran Church. Mühlenberg was a man of education and of exceptional organizing talent and was fully devoted to the cause to which he had given his life. Beginning his work in Pennsylvania in 1742, he soon brought the Lutheran congregations into some degree of order, infused into them "strong piety and a true church life," provided them with good pastors, and introduced schools for the education of children. His activities extended to all the Lutheran congregations in Pennsylvania, New York, New Jersey, and Maryland; and by the middle of the eighteenth century there were thirty thousand Lutherans in Pennsylvania alone, about four fifths of them being Germans. Another great event in Lutheran history was the formation in 1748 of the Synod of Pennsylvania, or, as it was called, "the Ministerium of North America." Mühlenberg was the instigator of this organization, though there were associated with him six other pastors and laymen from the several congregations. This may be truthfully called the most important event in eighteenth-century American Lutheran history.

The Mühlenbergs.—That the Lutherans had some part in winning independence is shown by the fact that two of the sons of the elder Mühlenberg, both of them Lutheran pastors, came to places of influence and leadership during and following the Revolution. Peter Mühlenberg became a general in the Revolutionary army. Frederick Augustus Mühlenberg was the first speaker of the national House of Representatives. Frederick Mühlenberg had been a member of the Continental Congress and later was president of the Pennsylvania convention that ratified the Constitution. The elder Mühlenberg had set a good example by preaching in Dutch, German, and English. He was broad and liberal in his views. He was friendly with the Reformed congregations. He welcomed Whitefield. Unfortunately, after his death, his example was not followed; and for a generation following the Revolution the American Lutherans made little progress largely because of too close adherence to the German language, the scarcity of ministers, and a want of leadership such as Mühlenberg had provided.

Organization of synods.—Following the Revolution several new synods were formed: the Ministerium or Synod of New York in 1786; the Synod of North Carolina in 1803; in 1818 the Synod of Ohio; in 1820, the Synods of Maryland and of Tennessee. In 1820 the first General Synod was organized, uniting four of the various State synods previously formed. This body remained the only general body of Lutherans in the United States until the Civil War.

Divisions from the General Synod.—The first division from the General Synod was occasioned by the Civil War. In 1862 the General Convention adopted a series of resolutions concerning and supporting the war for the Union, and this gave great offense to the Southern synods. The next year the Southern synods formed an organization known as the General Synod, South, which in 1886, with the Tennessee Synod, reorganized and took the name "United Synod of the South." A second division came in 1866 as a protest against the liberal tendency of the General Synod in interpreting the Augsburg Confession. This protest resulted in the formation of the General Council as a separate body.

Reunion of the three older bodies.—The three Lutheran groups—the General Synod, the United Synod of the South, and the General Council—representing the oldest Lutheran bodies in America, fortunately succeeded, in 1918, in coming together, and there was formed the United Lutheran Church. This church has a membership of more than eight hundred thousand members distributed among thirty-four synods. It is a nation-wide body, though its greatest strength is in Pennsylvania, New York, Maryland, and Ohio.

The newer Lutheran groups.—The rapid growth in the number of Lutherans in the United States within the last fifty years has been due in large measure to immigration from Lutheran countries. During the nineteenth century, after about 1850 especially, Germans, Swedes, Norwegians, Danes, and Finns came into the United States in great numbers and settled largely in the central and north-western section of the country. Here they have remained in communities, retained their native language, their church organization, and in many instances established parochial schools. Thus, the Augustana Synod, the most important Swedish Lutheran group, is a strong body with a large membership in the Central West. The Missouri Synod is largely German, as is also the Wisconsin Synod; and there are a Norwegian Synod, a Slovak Synod, and a Finnish Synod. Several of these newer groups have recently united into a loosely organized body known as the Synodical Conference, which has a membership somewhat larger than the United Lutheran Church. The Missouri Synod alone has a membership of more than seven hundred thousand.

Little unity among Lutheran groups.—There are more varieties of Lutherans in the United States than of any other sect, and they preach the gospel in more languages. Because many of the newer Lutheran groups

conduct their church services and their schools in a
foreign tongue they have been looked upon as a foreign
church, and during the Great War some of them were
accused of being un-American. In many instances, however, this was an unjust accusation. Due to the great
diversity among them, only a limited cooperation for common purpose has as yet been obtained. The Great War
did something to further cooperation among most of the
Lutheran bodies, and there was organized in 1919 a National Lutheran Council, which has concerned itself primarily with relief work in Europe. There is much yet
to be accomplished along the line of unity of effort, for the
extremes are still far apart.

Lutheran education in the United States.—The
Lutherans have always advocated and supported education, and the several Lutheran bodies in the United States
support many schools, colleges, and theological seminaries.
The United Lutheran Church maintains seventeen colleges
and thirteen theological seminaries. The Missouri Synod
has thirteen colleges and two theological seminaries, most
of them bearing the name "Concordia." The Swedish
Church supports nine colleges; the Norwegian Church,
four colleges and numerous academies. The newer Lutheran bodies have generally adopted the policy of maintaining parochial schools, where their children receive instruction in the native language. This fact brought them
under suspicion during the war, and many Lutheran
schools gave up the use of the foreign tongue in favor of
English. This practice, if continued, undoubtedly will
greatly benefit the Lutherans and will do much toward
removing suspicion of them among older American citi-
zens.

Lutheran contributions to American religious life.—
A Lutheran writer recently made the statement that "the
Lutheran Church has yet to make its greatest contribution to the religious life of America." This writer points
out that the chief contribution so far has been that of
a steadying and conservative force in American Protestantism. Like the Presbyterians the Lutherans have stood
steadily and sturdily by their ancient creed and their historic faith. Salvation through faith in Christ is central

in all Lutheran thinking. As a result of this emphasis Lutherans have not been greatly disturbed by such controversies as have rent other denominations, for they feel that their foundations are sure. Through all the years since the Diet of Augsburg until now Lutherans everywhere have grounded their faith upon the Augsburg Confession. And it is one of the glories of the Lutheran Church that it has always been careful to instruct its people and especially its children in Luther's *Smaller Catechism;* for "it believes that since it stands for a well-defined interpretation of the gospel, all its members should have the clearest possible conception of what that interpretation is." The Lutheran pastor considers such instruction as of equal importance with the sermon, and nothing has done more to maintain the inner unity of the Lutheran Church throughout the world than this instruction.

The Lutheran Church to-day.—The Lutheran Church is one of the largest Protestant bodies in America, standing third among the Protestant churches, with a membership of 2,500,000. It has been frequently misunderstood because of its large membership of foreign-speaking people; but none of the Lutheran churches in America is a branch of any European state church, and most Lutherans, especially those making up the United Lutheran Church, are thoroughly American and fully in sympathy with American ideals and institutions. "With the same robust faith exhibited by the man whose name it bears the Lutheran Church of our own day moves out singing with all its strength:

> " 'A mighty fortress is our God,
> A bulwark never failing.'

And it inscribes upon its banners those same great watchwords which have come down across the ages."

QUESTIONS FOR DISCUSSION

1. Who are the Lutherans, and what is their doctrinal position? How many Lutheran bodies are there in the

United States, and what have been the chief causes that have divided them into the several groups?

2. Describe the coming of the first Lutherans to America. How were Lutherans treated in New Amsterdam?

3. Where were the first Swedish Lutheran congregations in America?

4. Account for the great German migration to America in the early eighteenth century.

5. Tell of the work of Henry Melchior Mühlenberg among the Lutherans in America. What part did Mühlenberg's son take in the winning of independence and in the formation of the American government?

6. Describe the work of organization among the Lutherans following the gaining of independence.

7. What were the causes of division among the older Lutherans in America? Tell of their reunion.

8. What are some of the newer Lutheran groups in the United States? Why is unity so difficult to obtain among these newer Lutheran groups?

9. What have been the outstanding contributions made by the Lutherans to the religious life of America?

CHAPTER X

THE METHODISTS

WE have given some attention in a previous chapter to the beginnings of Methodism in England. We have noted how John Wesley and his associates formed the first Methodist societies, and how the movement grew, until by the last quarter of the eighteenth century Methodism had become a great factor in the religious and social life of England. In this chapter we propose to describe how Methodism came to America, how it became here an independent church, and how it grew to be the largest Protestant body in the United States.

Outstanding characteristics of Methodism.—In the first place, Methodism has never stood on a narrow doctrinal basis. When John Wesley abridged the Thirty-nine Articles of the English Church as a doctrinal basis for his societies he left out everything of a sectarian nature, so that they could be subscribed to by almost any evangelical Christian. He planned to establish a broad and generous platform on which all Christians, so far as possible, could unite. That he prescribed no mode of administering the sacraments of baptism and the Lord's Supper is typical of Wesley's whole attitude. Methodism also takes the broadest possible stand on matters of church government. It holds that the Scriptures prescribe no one type of church government, and that therefore no one type is of exclusive authority. It recognizes that any church is a true church if it is true to the spirit of the apostolic church.

Methodist emphasis upon experience.—As the Methodist movement arose as a protest against formalism, so naturally its dominant stress has been on inner experience. The distinctive Methodist emphasis falls upon at least three aspects of religious experience: conversion, sanctification, and the witness of the Spirit. By conversion is meant "a passage from moral deadness to moral life which profoundly affects the whole course of the life." By sanctification is meant the "extension of spiritual influences to all parts of a man's nature." Also, the Methodist, if he is true to type, "believes in an inner satisfaction of spiritual life which he calls assurance, or the witness of the Spirit." It is not to be understood, however, that Methodists claim any monopoly upon these emphases. Others have held to them also; nevertheless, these are the essentials of Methodism.

Religious training of children.—Although the early Methodist movement was characterized by warmth of emotion manifesting itself in great revivals, from the very first it laid particular stress upon the religious instruction and Christian nurture of children. Wesley was no mere revivalist, but was greatly concerned that the people called Methodists, especially the immature, should be gathered together for instruction and care. In a real sense this is the finest tradition of Methodism. "Above every influence it accounts for the amazing growth of the church throughout the earth and for the fact that to-day twenty million people count themselves followers of Christ under the leadership of John Wesley." One great board of the church, employing an increasing group of specialists, teachers, administrators, and field workers, concentrates on the one task of lifting the standards of religious education within the denomination to an adequate level. Moreover, by far the largest single output of the presses of The Methodist Book Concern is its religious-educational literature—a concrete evidence of Methodism's increasingly high regard for educational processes.

Methodism in America before the Revolution.—Methodism was introduced into the English colonies in America by two local preachers who began their work at about the same time. Philip Embury was an Irish local preacher who came to New York in 1760; but it was not until 1766, largely through the influence of Mrs. Barbara Heck, a relative, that he began to preach in his own house. Another Irish immigrant—Robert Strawbridge—who had come to Maryland began to preach at about the same time as Embury. The two Methodist societies growing out of their preaching, one in New York and the other in Maryland, were the first two Methodist societies in America. With the formation of these societies a request was sent to John Wesley that he send out missionaries to America. Wesley replied by sending Richard Boardman and Joseph Pilmoor in 1768. Three years later (1771) an additional missionary arrived in the person of Francis Asbury. In 1773 Thomas Rankin came out, having been named by Wesley as the superintendent of all the work in America, and in that year the first American conference convened in Philadelphia, which was attended by ten preachers, all of whom had been born in Ireland. Thus it was that Methodism in America began in the days just preceding the outbreak of the American Revolution. The preachers who had been sent to take charge of the work, having only recently come from England, had not had time fully to identify themselves with the American cause.

Methodism and the American Revolution.—At the outbreak of the Revolution there were 24 preachers and 4,921 members of Methodist societies in America. With the opening of hostilities all the preachers who had recently come from England returned except Francis Asbury, who deliberately made up his mind to identify himself with the Americans and their cause, though he refused to take the oath of allegiance in Maryland and was forced to flee to Delaware, where no oath was required of clergymen. In the first years of the war Methodism lost heavily, but soon extensive revivals began in several sections remote from the war, and the loss was soon overcome, so that by the end of the war there were eighty preachers and nearly fifteen thousand members in the Methodist societies in the United States.

Formation of the Methodist Episcopal Church.—At the close of the American Revolution, John Wesley determined, now that America was free, to make the Methodists in the United States independent of his authority. The American Methodists were without ordained ministers, for Francis Asbury himself had never been ordained; therefore, there were none who could administer the ordinances of baptism and the Lord's Supper. After failing in his attempt to get a bishop of the Established Church to ordain one of his preachers for America, Wesley concluded that he himself had the authority to ordain. Accordingly, he proceeded to ordain Richard Whatcoat and Thomas Vasey. He appointed Dr. Thomas Coke, already an ordained clergyman in the Church of England, superintendent. At the same time he drew up a form of service, made a collection of psalms and hymns, and sent Whatcoat, Vasey, and Coke across the Atlantic to organize the American Methodists into a new church. This was done at a Conference held in Baltimore, December 24, 1784, to January 2, 1785. At this Conference Asbury, who with Doctor Coke was to superintend the American church, was ordained deacon and elder and was elected general superintendent. Here also the name "Methodist Episcopal Church" was adopted.

Causes for the rapid growth of Methodism.—Due to the fact that the Methodists were ideally organized to meet the needs of a new country and to follow a moving population, Methodism made a remarkable growth during the early period of our national history. "Perhaps history has never seen a truer type of home missionary than the itinerant preachers of Methodism. Ready to obey orders like the Jesuits, strong to preach like the Dominicans, they went everywhere, threading forests, fording and swimming rivers, making friends with Indians or with chance settlers, traveling through parishes a hundred miles or more in extent, meeting their appointments with the regularity of machines, running the gantlet of all kinds of dangers." These Methodist itinerants preached a gospel of free, full, and present salvation at a time when the prevailing type of preaching in the other Protestant churches was Calvinistic. Their "emphasis on religious experience, personal knowledge of Christ, and victory over all sin gave both preachers and people a buoyant, triumphant life; and this sense of reality and power invested the pulpit with authority and fascination and its people with a vitalizing influence over others."

Progress of American Methodism in 1844.—Within five years after the formation of the Methodist Episcopal Church the number of preachers had more than doubled, and the membership had grown to more than fifty-seven thousand. The growth in the newer sections of the country was especially rapid. In 1800 the Western Conference was formed, embracing all the territory west of the Allegheny Mountains. At that time there were fewer than three thousand members in all the Western country; but twelve years later the membership in the Western Conference had passed the thirty-thousand mark. The number of preachers during the same period increased from ten to one hundred, and the number of circuits from nine to sixty-nine. While Methodism was penetrating into the new West it was at the same time gaining a foothold in New England. Here, led by Jesse Lee, one of the most interesting of the early Methodist preachers, the Methodists became well established in the very stronghold of Congregationalism. In these early years the bishops, as the superintendents had come to be called, traveled on horseback over the whole country, supervising the work from Maine to Georgia, and from the Atlantic to the most Western settlement, averaging in travel from four thousand to six thousand miles a year. By 1844 the Methodist Episcopal Church was perhaps the most evenly distributed church in America, with a membership of more than a million.

Beginnings of the church periodicals.—By the year 1844 several Methodist periodicals had been established. The Methodist Book Concern had been founded in New York City in 1789, and the Methodists were using the printing press to great advantage in supplying the people with religious books and papers. *Zion's Herald* had been established in Boston in 1826. Two years later *The Christian Advocate and Journal* began its weekly appearance in New York City, and in 1834 the *Western Christian Advocate* was begun in Cincinnati. Older than any of these, however, and oldest of the living periodicals of the church is the *Methodist Review,* the first issue dating back to the year 1818.

The slavery split in Methodism.—From the first Methodism had been opposed to slavery; and when the Methodist Episcopal Church was organized, Wesley's rule against slavery was accepted along with the others. But as the church grew and extended into the Southern States it came into contact more and more with slavery, and gradually the rules against slaveholding became less and less strict. Before it was hardly realized, numerous slaveholders were holding official positions in many Southern churches. Even ministers became the owners of slaves. Meanwhile there was growing up at the North a strong antislavery sentiment, and by about 1830 antislavery societies began to be formed among Methodist people, especially in the New England States. These antislavery people became very critical of the Methodist slaveholders, and as a natural result the Southerners came to be extremely sensitive and began very strongly to defend their position. A crisis was reached at the General Conference of 1844 over the fact that Bishop James O. Andrew, of Georgia, by a second marriage had become the owner of slaves. This fact, of course, would make Bishop Andrew unacceptable to the New England and other antislavery Conferences, and resolutions were passed asking Bishop Andrew to desist from exercising his authority as a bishop until he had rid himself of his slaves. The passage of this resolution caused a general feeling among the Southern Methodist leaders that it would be best for the church in the South to sever relations with the Methodist Episcopal Church. Accordingly, in 1845, there was organized in Louisville, Kentucky, a new church, which took the name "Methodist Episcopal Church, South."

Effect of the separation upon American Methodism.— From 1845 to the outbreak of the Civil War both the Methodist Episcopal Church and the Methodist Episcopal Church, South, grew rapidly. The Methodist Episcopal Church became more and more antislavery, while the Church, South, became a stanch defender of the institution of slavery, though making great efforts to take the message of Christianity to the slaves. So successful was their work among the Negroes that by 1860 there were more than 215,000 Negro Methodists in the Church, South. It is undoubtedly true that the separation in 1844, from the standpoint of increasing Methodist membership in the United States, was beneficial. A definite movement for unification of the two main branches of Methodism is under way. Since 1918 official groups representing both churches have been at work on various plans for a reunion of the people called Methodists. As this book is written the prospects are bright for a successful outcome of this unification movement, the 1924 General Conference of the Methodist Episcopal Church having adopted a plan of union by an almost unanimous vote.

Methodism and the Civil War.—The Methodist Episcopal Church rendered a great service to the country during the Civil War, for no church was more loyal to the government. When the war began, there was a total membership in the Methodist Episcopal Church of 990,447, and at the close of the war the membership had decreased by 61,188. President Lincoln said of the Methodist Episcopal Church during the Civil War: "Nobly sustained as the government has been by all the churches, I would utter nothing which might, in the least, appear invidious against any. Yet, without this, it may fairly be said that the Methodist Episcopal Church, not less devoted than the best, is, by its greater numbers, the most important of all. It is no fault in others that the Methodist Episcopal Church sent more soldiers to the field, more nurses to the hospitals, and more prayers to heaven than any." The Methodist Episcopal Church, South, gave an equal devotion to the cause of the Confederacy, and at the end of the war the Church South was depleted in membership and was greatly disorganized.

Changes in the church since the Civil War.—The church soon recovered from the effects of the Civil War, and there was a rapid growth in membership in the years immediately following, there being 222,687 more members in 1868 than there had been in 1864. Methodism kept pace with the advancing frontier and was especially firmly planted in the great prairie States of Kansas, Nebraska, and the Dakotas, at the same time more than holding her own in the mountain and Pacific States. Changes in the government of the church since the Civil War have been in the direction of making the church more democratic. In 1872 lay delegates were admitted to the General Conference, though it was not until 1900 that equal lay and ministerial representation was authorized. In

1904 women were admitted on an equal footing with men as lay delegates.

Connectional interests of the Methodist Episcopal Church.—The Methodist Episcopal Church carries on many lines of activity through various organizations. The most important of these are The Book Concern; the Boards of Foreign and Home Missions; the Board of Education, since 1924 including the departments of Schools and Colleges, Church Schools, Epworth League, and Education for Negroes; the Board of Conference Claimants; the Board of Hospitals and Homes and Deaconess Work; besides the Woman's Foreign and Home Missionary Societies. The names of these various boards describe the kinds of work they carry on. The Board of Foreign Missions and the Woman's Foreign Missionary Society, for example, conduct extensive missions the world round. Taken as a whole, there are no more efficient and effective organizations for the doing of these various tasks to be found anywhere in the world.

Methodists and education; early attempts.—Methodism was cradled at the ancient University of Oxford. From that time until now Methodism has been an increasing educational influence. Cokesbury College, planned by Bishops Asbury and Coke at Abingdon, Maryland, was the first Methodist educational institution in America. The corner stone was laid in 1785, but its career was abruptly ended in 1795 by a fire, which destroyed the only building. The untutored circuit riders of the West made the second attempt at founding a Methodist institution of learning and established Bethel Academy in Kentucky; but, due to poor location and the poverty of the country, it soon closed its doors. New England and New York Methodism has the honor of founding the first permanent Methodist schools—Wilbraham Academy, Cazenovia Seminary, and Genesee Wesleyan Seminary. By the year 1840 Methodist colleges and seminaries dotted the country, there being at that date twenty-seven seminaries and sixteen colleges under the control of the Methodist Episcopal Church.

The development of Methodist education in America.—Oldest among living Methodist colleges is Wesleyan University, Middletown, Connecticut, which was chartered in 1831. In rapid succession in the two decades following came McKendree College, Indiana Asbury (now DePauw University), Emory College, Ohio Wesleyan University, Allegheny College, Randolph-Macon College, and Dickinson College. Just before the Civil War, Northwestern University was established; and following the war Syracuse University and Boston University opened their doors. To-day there are forty-five colleges and universities, thirty-two secondary schools, and nineteen schools of various grades for Negroes under the control of the Methodist Episcopal Church alone. The Methodist Church, South, maintains twenty-nine colleges and universities and thirty junior colleges. More than one hundred million dollars is invested in Methodist educational institutions. The Methodist student body numbers more than one hundred thousand. Since 1873 the Board of Education of the Methodist Episcopal Church has assisted 34,162 Methodist students to obtain an education through its loan fund, and last year it made nearly three thousand loans aggregating $261,204. Nor is Methodist educational influence alone felt in Methodist colleges and universities. In the great nondenominational and State universities Methodist students far outnumber those of any other denominations, and Wesley foundations have been established in connection with these great universities for the religious care of students. No single group of people in America exercises a larger educational influence than do the Methodists.

The Methodist Episcopal Church, South.—At the formation of the Methodist Episcopal Church, South, in 1845, it had a membership of about 450,000 in twenty Conferences. With a few slight exceptions the Church South has had a history since the Civil War similar to that of the Methodist Episcopal Church. The Church South admits laymen to the Annual as well as to the General Conferences and has retained the time limit. The Church South maintains an extensive publishing house, with headquarters in Nashville, Tennessee, and supports numerous boards, such as the Boards of Foreign and Home Missions, the Board of Sunday Schools, the Board of Education and Church Extension. The Church South maintains twenty-seven colleges and two universities, besides numerous junior colleges and academies. It also maintains more than twenty periodicals and a *Quarterly Review.* The membership in the Church South for 1922 was 2,362,598, confined almost entirely to the Southern States.

Kinds of Methodists.—Altogether there are seventeen denominations that may be classed as Methodist, besides two other churches—the United Brethren and the Evangelical Churches—which may be classed as belonging to the Methodist family. Of these bodies nine are colored churches. Five of the white Methodist Churches are very small. Of the white Methodist Churches the Methodist Protestant is the largest outside of the two great branches —the Methodist Episcopal and the Methodist Episcopal Church, South. The three largest Negro churches are the African Methodist Episcopal, the African Methodist Episcopal Zion, and the Colored Methodist Episcopal; these three churches having a combined membership of more than 1,300,000. The total number of Methodists of all kinds in the United States, according to the numbers for the year 1922, was 8,262,289.

Methodist contributions to American religious life.— Methodism has contributed richly to the religious life of America. It has perhaps been the most successful church in meeting the needs of the advancing frontier and for that reason was the largest factor in shaping the ideals of the great Middle West particularly. The outstanding contributions of Methodism can be summed up as follows: *First,* Methodism has been characterized throughout its history by its splendid zeal. That zeal was found in Wesley and his contemporaries—a zeal which caused Wesley to rise every morning at four and fill every moment of a long life with a variety of Christian labors such as perhaps no other man has ever equaled. This same zeal has lived on in the church Wesley founded. It accounts for the vast labors of Asbury and McKendree, for the circuit riders on the frontier, who traveled circuits four hundred miles in length and preached every day in the week. It accounts also for the type of preaching which has come to be recognized as Methodistic—a type characterized by warmth and reality. *Secondly,* Methodism has contributed a sane emphasis upon emotion in religion, its leaders often declaring that primarily "religion is an emotion." This emphasis is shown in Methodist preaching and in Methodist hymns. Methodists, however, have never been content with simply an appeal to the emotions, but have in every instance "speedily harnessed these floods of emotion to some form of practical effort." *Thirdly,* Methodism has contributed a sense of the value of organization. Dean Charles R. Brown, of the Yale Divinity School, said recently, "I regard the polity of the Methodist Church as the best in the world, not even excepting the Roman Catholic." Methodism has had a large influence upon other churches. George Whitefield introduced a Methodist element into the evangelical churches during and following the Great Awakening, and that influence has continued until the present. Its type of evangelism has been widely adopted, while its form of organization not only has been largely copied by other churches, but has been effective in influencing the more loosely organized churches toward some kind of centralization. As a whole the liberal and catholic spirit of John Wesley has prevailed among American Methodists. Methodism was not at the beginning and has never been a doctrinal movement, and there have been few Methodist heresy trials and little theological warfare. American Methodists have retained to a large degree the buoyancy of spirit, the hopefulness, the energy, and the boldness that characterized their fathers. "By their splendid enthusiasm and zeal, by their wise and wide use of the emotional element in human nature, by their practical, efficient organization, they have made large and rapid growth." On the tomb of John Wesley in London are his own words: "The world is my parish," and "that body of Christians who revere him as the founder of their branch of the church has steadily moved ahead in splendid fulfillment of that great hope."

QUESTIONS FOR DISCUSSION

1. What are some of the outstanding characteristics of Methodism? What are the doctrines emphasized by the Methodists?

25060

2. Give an account of the introduction of Methodism in America. Who were Philip Embury, Robert Strawbridge, Richard Boardman, Joseph Pilmoor, and Francis Asbury?

3. Tell of the formation of the Methodist Episcopal Church in 1784. Who were Thomas Coke, Richard Whatcoat, and Thomas Vasey?

4. In what respects was Methodism ideally suited to meet the needs of a new country? When were the first Methodist periodicals established?

5. What was John Wesley's position on the question of slavery? How did the slavery question cause division in the Methodist Episcopal Church? What effect had the slavery division upon the growth of Methodism?

6. What part did the Methodist Episcopal Church take in the Civil War? What was the condition of the Methodist Episcopal Church, South, at the close of the war?

7. What have been the most important changes in the Methodist Episcopal Church since the Civil War?

8. What are the chief Methodist Churches besides the two main branches?

9. What have been Methodism's outstanding contributions to the religious life of America?

10. What ways has Methodism affected the other Protestant churches in America?

CHAPTER XI

THE PRESBYTERIANS

JUST as the Lutherans represent those Christians who follow most closely the teachings of Martin Luther, so the Presbyterians are those Christians who follow most closely the great reformers Zwingli and Calvin. In the broadest sense all those churches which are ruled by presbyters or elders are presbyterian.

Presbyterian doctrine.—Not only do Presbyterians follow John Calvin in matters of church government: they are thoroughgoing Calvinists in their theology. The Presbyterian Church has been called a doctrinal church, for it puts great emphasis upon doctrine and demands of its ministers and ruling elders exacting assent to its confessions of faith. The great Presbyterian statement of doctrine is the Westminster Confession, drawn up in the famous Westminster Abbey in the year 1643, at the time when the Puritan party had gained supremacy in England. The Confession is a digest of the system of doctrine taught by John Calvin. It proclaims the complete sovereignty of God in the universe, the complete sovereignty of Christ in salvation, the sovereignty of the Scriptures in faith and conduct, and the sovereignty of the individual conscience in the interpretation of the Word of God. Summed up briefly, Calvinism teaches that man is hopelessly corrupt, that his salvation depends on his unconditional election, that Christ died for the elect only, that no one elected to salvation can successfully resist, and the final perseverance of the saints—"once in grace always in grace." It was upon this stern statement that the Presbyterian Church took its stand—a creed "designed to build up a massive and masculine type of piety in the lives of those who give it their adherence."

Calvinism a reaction from the teachings of the medieval church.—It is important to bear in mind that all the churches which came out of the Reformation were Calvinistic in their theology. And this was only natural. The medieval church taught that the salvation of people lay entirely in the hands of the church, while Calvin taught that the basis of all Christian faith was the Word of God and the absolute dependence of all things on God himself immediately and directly. In other words, Calvin emphasized the importance of God in man's salvation as contrasted to the teaching of the church that salvation lay in obedience to her.

Presbyterianism in Europe at the opening of the colonial period.—At the beginning of the colonial period there were numerous groups of Presbyterians in the countries of Western Europe as well as in England, Scotland, and north Ireland. By the end of the sixteenth century the system of John Calvin had been established in Switzerland, France, Germany, and the Netherlands, and from the reign of Edward VI (1547–53) Presbyterian principles and ideas were making headway in England. The most important stronghold of Presbyterianism from the standpoint of America, however, was in Scotland and the north of Ireland, for it was from these two sources that the majority of Presbyterians in the colonies came. By the opening of the seventeenth century the Presbyterian had become the state church of Scotland, and during the reigns of Elizabeth and James I Scotch colonists brought Presbyterianism to the north of Ireland. Thus we see how Presbyterianism had been established in many places in the Old World at the time America was being colonized, and it is thus easy to understand how the several groups of Presbyterians came to America. From Holland came the Dutch Reformed, from Germany and Switzerland came the German Reformed, from England came English Presbyterians, from Scotland came the several kinds of Scotch Presbyterians, and from north Ireland came the Scotch-Irish, who were to be found so numerously in the western part of the country at the opening of the Revolution.

Presbyterianism in the colonies.—In the middle colonies the most important religious element were the Calvinistic denominations, such as the German and Dutch Reformed, and the English and Scotch-Irish Presbyterians. In New England there was not much distinction between the Congregationalists and the Presbyterians. There were several Huguenot churches established by the French in New York, Charleston, and even in Massachusetts. From about 1730 to the opening of the Revolution the Presbyterian element in the colonies grew rapidly, especially in central and western Pennsylvania, and in western Virginia and the Carolinas, due to the large Scotch-Irish immigration. The first American presbytery was organized in 1706 in Philadelphia, and by 1717 a synod of four presbyteries was formed.

The effect of the Great Awakening on the Presbyterians.—We have already noticed some of the effects of the Great Awakening upon the colonial churches and we have seen how the Presbyterians, like the Congregationalists, were divided over the revival. There soon developed two parties within the Presbyterian church, the stricter party demanding conformity to the old standards, while the liberal party favored the revival methods of the Tennents and Whitefield. The result of the contest between the two parties was the formation in 1745 of a new synod—that of New York—which was made up of the liberal element. The Philadelphia Synod was called the Old Side, while the New York Synod was known as the New Side.

The establishment of Princeton.—Soon after the formation of the New Side Synod the College of New Jersey was established at Elizabethtown (1747) and the Log College of the Tennents was merged into it. In 1755 the institution was moved to Princeton. The New Side party reaped all the benefits from the Great Awakening and accordingly grew much more rapidly than did the Old Side. In fact, the Philadelphia Synod actually decreased, while the Synod of New York grew within a few years from twenty to seventy-two ministers. Finally, the differences between the two parties were largely overcome, and the two synods were united in 1758. This union brought great prosperity to the College of New Jersey at Princeton under the leadership of President John Witherspoon.

The Presbyterians and the Revolutionary War.—The Presbyterians in the colonies were as a rule patriots and gave unstinted devotion to the cause of independence. John Witherspoon was the only minister who was a member of the Continental Congress when the Declaration of Independence was adopted; and other Presbyterian leaders, such as Daniel Morgan and Andrew Pickens of the Carolinas, both of whom were Presbyterian elders, were prominent in the war in the South. At the frontier battles of King's Mountain and Cowpens, Presbyterian backwoodsmen were the backbone of the American forces. At the close of the war the Presbyterians were badly disorganized, but their recovery was rapid. In 1788 the Synod of New York and Philadelphia decided to form a General Assembly, and at the assembly's first meeting in 1789 the Westminster Confession was revised and adopted, as well as a book of discipline, and the Presbyterian Church in the United States was started upon its independent career.

Divisions in the Presbyterian Church.—The Presbyterian Church in the United States has suffered at least three serious divisions. The first came about during the early years of the nineteenth century and was due to the great revival that swept over the Western country from about 1795 to 1805. We have already described in another chapter the effect of the revival upon the Presbyterian Church and the events that led to the formation of the Cumberland Presbyterian Church in 1810. The new church grew rapidly, especially in the border States, where it had originated. The new church adopted the Westminster Confession with the omission of its stern Calvinism and declared the free agency of man. In government, however, it remained purely presbyterian. A second division came in 1837, brought about over doctrinal questions, especially the doctrine of the atonement, and resulted in the formation of the Old School and the New School bodies. A third division resulted from the slavery controversy and the outbreak of the Civil War. In 1858 the New School churches in the South separated on the question of slavery, and in 1861 the Old School churches in the South followed. At the close of the war (1865) they united in what is now the Southern Presbyterian Church.

The Old School and the New School churches at the North followed the example of the churches in the South and united in 1869.

The Reformed Churches in the United States.—The Swiss, Dutch, and German Churches, which trace their origin back to Calvin and Zwingli, came to be known as Reformed. The Reformed Church in America, known as the Dutch Reformed until 1867, was brought to America by the Dutch colonists in and around New York. This church is presbyterian in church polity. It has 141,222 members and is strongest in New York, Michigan, and Illinois. The Reformed Church in the United States was formerly known as the German Reformed. The first members of this church founded Germantown, and many more came to America during the eighteenth century. To-day this church numbers 337,526 members and is strongest in Pennsylvania. The principal colleges under the control of the Reformed Church in the United States are Franklin and Marshall, at Lancaster, Pennsylvania; Heidelberg, at Tiffin, Ohio; and Ursinus, at Collegeville, Pennsylvania.

Other Presbyterian bodies.—Still another Presbyterian church of considerable importance is the United Presbyterian Church of North America. This church is made up of a union of several branches of Scotch Presbyterians—a union that was consummated in 1858. It is an extremely conservative body, with a membership of 162,780. Altogether there are nine Presbyterian and three Reformed Churches in the United States. The total Presbyterian membership is 2,402,392. The total Reformed membership is 525,161.

Distinctive features of the Presbyterians.—The Presbyterian Church is one of the great churches of America, and no single body has made more distinctive contributions to the religious life of the nation. It is a "close-knit, highly organized body standing midway between the monarchical form of church government by bishops and the pure democracy of the congregational polity." It has always stood for very definite things and it has always stood by its guns. In a recent book by Dean Charles R. Brown, of the Yale Divinity School, the contributions of nine of the American churches to the religious life of

America have been admirably set forth, and I can do no better here than summarize his estimate of the contribution of the Presbyterian Church.

The Presbyterian Church as a conservative influence.— Through all the years the Presbyterian Church has steadily stood by the Westminster Confession of Faith. Thus, Presbyterianism is firmly grounded in the past. For that reason it is not easily stampeded. "It has a conservative habit of mind." It is quite the custom in these days to make fun of our ancient creeds, and it is very easy for those who are so inclined to find flaws in the Presbyterian confession of faith, just as it is easy to find flaws, in the light of modern thinking, in the Apostles' Creed. But, judged by its fruits, by the type of men and women who have lived and died by it, it is not easy to find another creed that can stand comparison with the Westminster Confession. No Protestant church has stood more stanchly by its doctrines than has the Presbyterian, which accounts for the fact that the most famous of modern heresy trials have taken place within the Presbyterian Church. In this twentieth century we are accustomed to say that doctrine and creed do not count, that it makes very little difference what a man believes; but the Presbyterian Church has always said that it does make a difference. When a host of professing Christians are saying that they do not know what they believe, it is heartening to know that here is a great body of faithful, sturdy Christian men and women who do know what they believe and are determined to hold fast that which they have, through the years, proved to be good.

Presbyterian emphasis upon the enormity of sin.—The habit of making light of and minimizing sin is altogether too common in these days; but, however much of this sort of thing there may be, this much is sure: the Presbyterian Church has not contributed to it. The Presbyterian Church has always been strongly Calvinistic in this respect: it has never underestimated the awfulness of wrongdoing; it has never painted black white; it has never taught that "the sinner will naturally and easily grow up out of his sin into the goodness of a saint by a process of evolution." Calvinism pictured the race as lost in sin, beyond all possibility of redemption except through the power of God. It is out of this overwhelming sense of sin that the highest morality in the world has developed, and in these days of laxity in morals and life we can well be glad for such a group of faithful people as make up the great Presbyterian Church—people who are not in the habit of minimizing the weakness and wrongdoing of the race.

Devotion to the Bible and insistence upon an educated ministry.—The Presbyterian Church has always been distinguished for "painstaking and profound scholarship," and none has done more to exalt the study of the Bible. Out of this exaltation of Bible study has come the insistence that her ministers shall be fully qualified by education and training properly to preach the Word. For more than a hundred years the Presbyterian Church has insisted that candidates for her ministry shall be college-bred men and for many years has insisted on seminary training in addition. This perhaps has given the Presbyterian Church the best prepared ministry, from the standpoint of the schools, at least, in America. This attitude of the church toward Bible study and adequately trained ministers has reacted upon raising the standard of Bible study among the members. The Presbyterian Church has made much of the religious training of children in the home. It has never stressed the emotional in religion, but, rather, the slower and perhaps the surer process of Christian nurture through education. It has come to my attention more than once that children brought up in good Presbyterian homes honor the Word of God and are able to repeat large sections from it. "In these days, when critical study and the purely literary treatment of the Bible have been unsettling the faith of many and have been lowering the Bible in the estimation of others, this supreme honor placed upon the Word of God by this branch of the church has been of inestimable worth."

QUESTIONS FOR DISCUSSION

1. What is understood by Calvinistic doctrine? In what sense was John Calvin the founder of Presbyterian-

ism? Why were all the churches which came immediately out of the Reformation Calvinistic in their theology?

2. What was the extent of Presbyterianism in Europe at the beginning of English colonization?

3. Where were the Presbyterian most numerous in the colonies? What effect had the Great Awakening upon the Presbyterians? Where did the Scotch-Irish settle in America?

3. Where were the Presbyterians most numerous in the Revolution?

5. Account for the rise of the Cumberland Presbyterian Church; for the Presbyterian Church, South. What is meant by the Old School and the New School?

6. What is the origin of the Reformed Churches in the United States? Explain the origin of the United Presbyterian Church.

7. In what respect has the Presbyterian Church been a steadying and conservative influence. What have been some of the other distinctive contributions of the Presbyterians?

CHAPTER XII

THE DISCIPLES, THE UNITED BRETHREN, AND THE SOCIETY OF FRIENDS

THE churches we are to consider in this chapter are the Disciples, the United Brethren, and the Society of Friends. The only reason for this grouping is the fact that these three are the most important of the churches not yet considered.

THE DISCIPLES OF CHRIST

The origin of the Disciples.—This is the youngest of the larger denominations in the United States, having come out of the great Western revival at the beginning of the last century. The church had a dual origin. Barton W. Stone, a Presbyterian minister of Kentucky, who had been prominent in the revival, withdrew from his church in 1804 and formed a society with no creed but the Bible and with no name other than Christian. At about the same time a similar movement was under way in western Pennsylvania, fathered by Thomas Campbell and his son Alexander, both Presbyterian ministers who had recently come from Ireland. The elder Campbell had begun to preach in a Presbyterian church in western Pennsylvania, but his liberality in inviting outsiders to a communion service brought censure upon him, and he withdrew from the Presbyterian Church. With his son he began to organize union societies. Having no desire to form a new church, they sought to unite with the Baptists; but after a few years they were forced out of this fellowship. Finding the necessity of forming a new communion inevitable, and since the aims of the two movements were similar, they undertook negotiations with Stone, looking toward union with his movement. This union was eventually consummated in 1827.

The names "Christians" and "Disciples of Christ."—On

the formation of this union the question arose as to the name of the new church. Stone favored the name "Christian"; Campbell was partial to the name "Disciples of Christ." As a result of this difference of opinion between the two leaders no definite name was then chosen, and for many years the denomination was known by both names —a fact that has caused considerable confusion. Recently, however, an international convention has chosen the name "Disciples of Christ" as the official name, though, as a matter of fact, there is no official name.

Rapid growth of the Disciples.—Throughout the Middle West—especially in those States where the movement had its origin and in neighboring States—the Disciples Church has had a rapid growth. In their church organization they were very democratic, adopting the congregational form of church polity—a fact that has contributed to their popularity in the Middle West. The Civil War caused the church to suffer greatly, since it was strongest in the border States. The church rapidly recovered from the effects of the war, however, and became the strong competitors with the Baptists and the Methodists in many a community. To-day the Disciples number 1,218,849 members in the United States.

The leading principles of the Disciples.—The outstanding principles of the Disciples have been summed up as follows: (1) "to restore the lost unity of believers and so of the Church of Christ by a return in doctrine, ordinance, and life to the religion definitely outlined in the New Testament; (2) no human creed, but the Bible only as the rule of faith and practice; (3) baptism by immersion of believers only, in which 'comes a divine assurance of remission of sins and acceptance with God'; (4) the celebration of the Lord's Supper as a 'feast of love' every Sunday."

The Disciples Church an outgrowth of an attempt at Christian union.—The Disciples developed into a separate church against the wishes of their leaders. In fundamentals the Campbells agreed with other evangelical Christians and they sought to eliminate those things on which Christians differ and to unite about those principles on which there is universal agreement. They had no de-

sire to form a new creed but, rather, sought to lead the
way out of denominational confusion. They therefore
chose a catholic name—"Christians," or "Disciples"—a
name about which there could be no difference of opinion.
They did not seek to compromise on the matter of creed,
but simply asked for the acceptance of the Lordship of
Jesus Christ. As to doctrine they asked that all agree to
accept the Scriptures. On the matter of baptism there
was a struggle, but finally they agreed on that mode that
is recognized by all Christians—namely, immersion. Both
Stone and the Campbells had been Presbyterians and as
such had accepted sprinkling as a mode of baptism, but
on adopting immersion they recognized the fact that many
earnest people could not accept sprinkling, while all recognized immersion as a valid mode. This was the platform upon which the Disciples sought to bring about
Christian union. It was no doubt a source of great disappointment to the leaders of the movement that instead
of bringing church union nearer they succeeded only in
creating another denomination; yet the fact that a hundred years ago earnest Christian men did prayerfully seek
to bring about unity among the churches has undoubtedly
had its influence for good.

Contributions of the Disciples.—The Disciples Church
has proved that it is possible to have an effective and
united Christian body without a man-made creed. No
denomination exceeds the Disciples in their denominational consciousness, yet there are those who insist that a
creedless church is a rope of sand. The fact, also, that
they have no creedal statements has allowed a large measure of intellectual freedom among them, and they have
had, as a result, few if any heresy trials. The Disciples
have always set an example for Bible study. Alexander
Campbell led the way in advocating the modern view of
the Scriptures and placed a different value upon the Old
and New Testaments at a time when many church leaders
were insisting that every book in the Bible was of equal
value. Throughout their one hundred years of history the
Disciples have likewise maintained a steady and effective
evangelism—a fact that in large measure accounts for
their large and aggressive membership.

The United Brethren in Christ

William Philip Otterbein.—There is a considerable similarity between the experience of William Philip Otterbein, the founder of the United Brethren Church, and that of John Wesley. Otterbein came to America from southern Germany in 1752 and began missionary work among the German Reformed people of Pennsylvania. While engaged in this work he went through an inner experience quite similar to that of Wesley when he felt his heart "strangely warmed." From this time on Otterbein laid great emphasis in his preaching on inner spiritual experience—a fact that offended some of his people as well as his colleagues. At about the same time he came in touch with Martin Boehm, a Mennonite who had passed through a similar experience, and together they conducted evangelistic work among the scattered settlers of Pennsylvania and neighboring colonies. This activity greatly offended the German Reformed ministers—so much so that Otterbein decided to accept a call to minister to an independent congregation in Baltimore, where he began his work in 1774.

Formation of the United Brethren Church.—Meanwhile Otterbein continued his evangelistic tours among the German-speaking people of the surrounding States, at the same time keeping in touch with Martin Boehm. By this time Otterbein had formed a close personal friendship with Francis Asbury; and when, in 1784, Asbury was ordained at the Christmas Conference in Baltimore, Otterbein was present and assisted in the ordination. Gradually there came to be a number of preachers (most of them from the German Reformed Church) who were in sympathy with Otterbein, and these ministers met occasionally in informal conferences, the first such conference being held in Baltimore in 1789. It is very probable that if the Methodists, following the Revolution, had made adequate provision for work among German-speaking people, Otterbein and those cooperating with him might have united with the Methodist Episcopal Church. Unfortunately no such provision was made; and in 1800 Otterbein, Boehm, and eleven others felt it necessary to form a new church, which the founders called the United Brethren in Christ. The name was derived from the greeting "We are brethren," which Otterbein had extended to Boehm after hearing him preach for the first time.

Government and doctrine.—Emphasizing the experience of conversion and having adopted the methods in vogue among the Methodists (and due perhaps also to the personal friendship between Asbury and Otterbein), the United Brethren adopted a form of church government which was a duplication of that of the Methodist Episcopal Church. They are Arminian in doctrine, emphasizing sanctification. In regard to baptism and the Lord's Supper they prescribe no set mode of administering, the choice of mode being left to the individual, as is also true of foot washing, which is sometimes practiced.

Growth and distribution.—For some years following the organization of the United Brethren Church work was carried on mainly among German-speaking people; but gradually congregations of English-speaking people were gathered, and to-day the bulk of the membership is English-speaking. With the Western movement of population into the Ohio and Mississippi valleys preaching places were established in Ohio, Indiana, and Illinois; and to-day the largest membership is to be found in the Central States and Pennsylvania. The United Brethren have practically no churches in the South, though they have spread westward to the Pacific Coast. Like most of the American churches the United Brethren have suffered a division. In 1889 a new constitution was adopted over the protest of a strong minority. The conservative minority refused to accept the new constitution and decided to remain under the old, claiming to be the true United Brethren Church. This caused some bitter contests over church property and some hard feelings which time has largely obliterated. The church holding to the revised constitution is by far the stronger, numbering 370,628 members, while the conservative branch has fewer than twenty thousand. The total membership of both is 389,972.

Contributions of the United Brethren.—Many of the reform movements characteristic of the Methodist Churches have found ready acceptance among the United Brethren.

Indeed, they have led the way in many reforms. They took an early stand against the manufacture and sale of intoxicating liquor. Their condemnation of slavery came in 1821, more than twenty years before the Methodists had reached their rightful position on that question. The United Brethren have been able to carry out numerous reforms that larger denominations have been unable to accomplish. Thus, they were among the first to ordain women and to admit laymen into their lawmaking bodies and annual conferences. They are an extremely earnest and devoted people and, through pulpit and press, have accomplished extensive and useful work. To an outsider, however, there does not seem enough difference between the United Brethren and the Methodist group of churches to warrant their continued separate existence.

The Society of Friends, or the Quakers

We have already given some attention (in Chapter II) to the origin of the Society of Friends in England under the preaching of George Fox, and we have seen how the great Quaker colonies in America were established largely through the efforts of William Penn. It remains now to trace the development of the Society of Friends from the colonial period to the present and to estimate their contribution to the religious life of America.

Quaker doctrine.—The Quakers have never adopted a formal creed, but in essential points they accept the fundamental positions of the great body of Christians. The most distinctive features of their faith are: (1) "the great importance attached to the immediate personal teaching of the Holy Spirit, or 'light within' or 'inner light'; (2) the absence of all outward ordinances, including baptism and the Lord's Supper, on the ground that they are not essential, were not commanded by Christ, and, moreover, tend to draw the soul away from the essential to the non-essential and formal; (3) the manner of worship and appointment of ministers" (in the public worship of the Quakers periods of silence often occur when each individual is in communion with God); (4) "the doctrine of peace, or nonresistance, in accordance with which no Friend can fight or directly support war."

Quaker organization.—The individual society or congregation is called a meeting, and their houses of worship meetinghouses. A number of local meetings make up the monthly meeting, while the quarterly meeting is composed of a group of monthly meetings. Above the quarterly meeting is the yearly meeting. In 1902 thirteen of the yearly meetings in the United States formed a five years' meeting, the purpose of which was to consider matters common to all and to provide a means for better cooperation in such work as might be undertaken in common, such as missions, temperance, peace propaganda, and work among Indians and Negroes.

Divisions among the Quakers.—The nineteenth century saw the Quakers divided into four groups—the Orthodox, the Hicksite, the Wilburite, and the Primitive. The Hicksite group separated in 1827 because of the teachings of Elias Hicks, a Quaker preacher of great earnestness who emphasized "obedience to the light within" in such a way that he was accused of being more or less in sympathy with Unitarian views. The Wilburite division came in 1845 under the leadership of John Wilbur, who objected to the new methods adopted to carry on evangelistic and missionary work in the West. The Primitive group is very small and is practically Wilburite in everything except maintaining a separate organization. The Orthodox Friends are by far the most numerous, with a membership of 85,612. The total membership of all bodies of the Friends in the United States is only 106,545.

Contributions of the Quakers.—Philip Schaff, perhaps the greatest of American church historians, once wrote the following concerning the Society of Friends: "The Society of Friends, though one of the smallest tribes in Israel, is a glorious society; for it has borne witness to the inner light which 'lighteth every man that cometh into the world'; it has proved the superiority of the Spirit over all forms; it has done noble service in promoting tolerance and liberty, in prison reform, the emancipation of slaves, and other works of Christian philanthropy." A recent writer on the Quakers has summed up their contributions to religion under the following heads: First, their emphasis upon worship through silence. In most of our

Protestant churches there is too much talking. The average minister is apt to force his service, feeling that a pause is a let-down. Certainly the Quaker emphasis in worship can be effectively utilized by other churches, especially in this day when men and women are apt to be nervous and distraught. A second contribution is their mysticism. In these days when the emphasis is all upon scientific explanation, the Quaker continues to emphasize communion with the Holy Spirit; the leadings of the inner light. The Quakers are perhaps the purest mystics we have among us, and their example and their teaching we could ill afford to do without. They have made large contributions also because of their social passion. The Quaker mystic has not alone been occupied in contemplation of the mysterious forces all about him, but has constantly concerned himself with the happiness and peace of mankind. This accounts for the leadership of the Quakers in the antislavery crusade, when the Quaker poet John Greenleaf Whittier sang his songs of freedom; in prison reform and in relief work among the poor and needy, which they are even now carrying on in the war-torn countries of Europe. Then, the Quakers have exercised an influence far greater than their numbers would indicate in their advocacy of peace. The pacifism of the Quaker has been defined not as an act, but, rather, it is his very character. "The Quaker thinks peace; it is his life."

QUESTIONS FOR DISCUSSION

1. Explain the origin of the Disciples Church. Why is the name "Christian" Church often applied to this body?

2. What are the leading principles of the Disciples Church? In what respect can we say that the Disciples Church is an outgrowth of an attempt at Christian unity?

3. What are some of the distinctive contributions of the Disciples?

4. Describe the career of William Philip Otterbein. What was Otterbein's relation to Francis Asbury?

5. When and why did Otterbein form a new church? Why did this church adopt the Methodistic form of church

government? Where are the United Brethren most numerous in the United States?

6. Name some of the distinctive contributions made by the United Brethren.

7. What are the distinctive features of the Quakers, or Friends?

8. Explain how the Friends carry on their church government.

9. What are some of the great reform movements in which the Quakers have taken a leading part?

10. Discuss some of the outstanding contributions made by the Friends to the religious life of America.

CHAPTER XIII

CHURCH FEDERATION AND UNION

NOWHERE in the world have there been more divisions in the church than in America. The fundamental reason for this is the fact that nowhere else has individualism been so highly developed. The Reformation freed the individual from the age-long domination of the Roman Catholic Church. Immediately thereafter the individual reformers, such as Luther, Zwingli, and Calvin, to mention only the three most conspicuous, began to differ in their interpretations of the teachings of the New Testament. Many of these differences, which had developed in Europe and in England after the Reformation, were brought over by the various groups of colonists who migrated to America.

Causes for further division in the colonial period.— When the several religious groups arrived in America, instead of uniting with others and forgetting their religious differences they tended to become even more distinct and individualistic; for, as a rule, after arriving in America they were located far apart, with little opportunity of contact with one another. The pioneer is always an independent individualist, as a rule, determined to go his own way as far as possible. Arriving in America, they found there no ancient traditions, no age-long customs, no high church officials to hold them into line ecclesiastically, and the result was multiplication of sects and churches. The attempt to form a state church in several of the colonies provoked even more division, for many had come to America to avoid that very arrangement.

Some factors working for a closer relation among the churches in the colonial period.— Although the colonial period furnished many causes for division among the churches, there were present some forces working toward a better understanding and closer relationships. One such

118

force was the common experiences of the pioneers. They were all engaged in the same kind of struggle, meeting daily the same dangers, the same tasks, and the same sorrows. They likewise all felt the responsibility of planting Christianity firmly in the New World. There was little disagreement on the fundamental doctrines among the colonial churches; their chief differences arose mainly over questions of church government. One great result that came out of the existence of the numerous sects in the colonial period was mutual toleration and the recognition of one another's equality before the law. Without this influence, which grew stronger as the Revolution approached, there could not have been written into the Constitution the guaranties of religious freedom. Perhaps the greatest unifying influence of the colonial period came out of the Great Awakening and the preaching of George Whitefield—a fact we have already noticed in a former chapter. By the end of the colonial era there had come to be certain principles recognized by practically all the sects. These were (1) separation of church and state; (2) equality of the churches before the law; (3) religious toleration—three great principles that have come to be considered as a part of the Constitution of democracy everywhere.

Causes of division among the churches since independence.—We may summarize the main causes for division among the churches in America since independence under the following heads: (1) revivals; (2) slavery and secession; (3) doctrine; (4) church rites and practices; (5) church government. The great revivals that have swept over the American churches from time to time have had both a unifying and a divisive effect. We have already noticed how the Great Awakening divided churches in New England into the New Lights and the Old Lights. The Presbyterians were split into the Old Side and the New Side, the latter favoring the revival and its methods, and the former becoming extremely bitter in its opposition. Again, in the great Western revival the Presbyterians suffered another split, and the Cumberland Presbyterian Church was the result. The United Brethren and the Evangelical Churches both came about over the revival influences exerted by Methodism on the German Reformed and the Lutheran Churches. The leaders and most of the original members of the United Brethren and Evangelical churches were drawn largely from the older German churches, which were opposed to the revival methods. Slavery and secession have been the fruitful causes of several great schisms, the Methodist Episcopal, the Presbyterian, the Baptist, and the Lutheran being the principal churches that suffered thereby. The chief divisions created over doctrinal differences are the Unitarian split in the Congregational Church, the Arminian division in the Baptist Church, the Universalist movement, and the division in the Society of Friends into the Hicksite and Orthodox. One of the causes of the separation of the Cumberland Presbyterians was their opposition to the old strict Calvinism and their leaning toward the Arminian position. A fourth reason for church division has been the question of church practices and rites. The Baptists have divided over the laying on of hands; the Dunkers over the question of Sabbath observances; others over foot washing. The Reformed Episcopal Church arose over the administering of the communion by an Episcopal clergyman in a Presbyterian church. The Disciples Church was formed largely around a mode of administering baptism. A fifth cause of division has been the matter of church government. Thus, the Methodist Protestant Church arose over the question of the appointing power of the bishops. One of the reasons for the formation of the Methodist Episcopal Church, South, was a difference of opinion over the question of the jurisdiction of the General Conference over the bishops. To-day many of these divisions seem to us to have been unjustifiable, but at the time they occurred the leaders of these separations were undoubtedly sincere and loyal to what they considered the highest good of the Kingdom. Undoubtedly they were men of conviction, and we can respect their motives, although we may at the same time deplore the divisions they were largely responsible for creating.

The movement for church union.—It is now our task to consider some of the movements looking toward church union. The history of Protestantism has to do too largely with division, but within recent years movements looking toward church cooperation and union have got under way, promising great things for the Protestantism of the future.

Early interdenominational movements within the United States.—The story of the beginning of church cooperation in the United States begins about a hundred years ago. In the year 1801 the Congregational and Presbyterian churches agreed upon a "Plan of Union" for carrying on Christian work in the West. The formation of the American Board of Commissioners for Foreign Missions (1814) was another step in practical cooperation by the same churches. Two years later a further step was taken in the organization of the American Bible Society, which was formed by a group of delegates representing the Baptist, Congregational, Episcopalian, Friends, Reformed, and Presbyterian Churches, later joined by the Methodists and several other denominations. The labors of this society in furnishing Bibles at first to the people in the new West and later to people of every race and tongue in the world, have been equally helpful to all the churches, and the work of the society has continued with ever-increasing usefulness to the present day.

Revival movements as an influence for union.—Many of the great revival movements that have swept over the United States from time to time have been of an undenominational character. The great Western revival (1797—1805) was of this nature. Other revivals, such as that centering about the work of President Charles F. Finley of Oberlin College (1857–58) and the evangelistic movements fathered by Dwight L. Moody, were to a great extent undenominational movements. The modern revivals are more and more of an undenominational character and have had considerable unifying influence among the churches.

Young Men's and Young Women's Christian Associations.—There has been no influence for unifying Christian people greater than that exercised by the Young Men's and Young Women's Christian Associations. The Young Men's Christian Association grew out of the labors of a young Englishman—George Williams. Williams had been converted as a boy of fifteen. Coming up to London in

1841 and finding employment in an establishment where there were numerous young clerks, he set out to form a group of these young men for the purposes of prayer and Bible study. This became the nucleus of the Y. M. C. A. It was in 1844 that this group was organized, and within a few weeks it was determined to extend the work of the organization to all young men in London, and the name "Young Men's Christian Association" was adopted. By 1851 the movement had spread to the United States, and the first association was begun at Boston. From this small beginning the society rapidly spread throughout the United States and, in more recent years, throughout the world. Men of all Christian creeds have joined in its association, and it has been a great boon not alone to young men everywhere but to the organized church as well. The Young Women's Christian Association dates from 1858, when an association called the Ladies' Christian Association was formed in New York. Similar associations were organized in several of the Eastern cities, and in 1866 the Boston Association took the name "Young Women's Christian Association." It was not long before the association had taken root in Cincinnati, Cleveland, and Saint Louis and it is now to be found in every city of any size in the country. Like the Y. M. C. A. it has developed into a world association, and its ministries of helpfulness are extended to multitudes without regard to creed.

The student movement.—Closely related to the Y. M. and Y. W. C. A. is the student movement. The first student Y. M. C. A. was formed in 1858, and in 1872 the first student Y. W. C. A. appeared. These organizations are now to be found in practically every college and university in the United States outside of the Roman Catholic institutions, and they exert a powerful influence in the building of Christian character. The Student Volunteer Movement was inspired by Dwight L. Moody as early as 1886, and an outgrowth of this movement was the World's Student Christian Federation, formed in 1895, which aimed to unite the various student movements in all lands, to foster relations among them, to collect information regarding religious conditions among students everywhere, to promote a deeper spiritual life among students, and to enlist students in the work of extending the Kingdom.

Laymen's and young people's movements.—Movements among laymen have been more or less numerous in recent years. The Laymen's Missionary Movement, starting in 1906, was among the first. This was an attempt to create a larger interest among laymen in foreign missions. Of like nature was the Men and Religion Forward Movement, which was begun about 1912 for the purpose of enlisting laymen to a larger degree in the whole activity of the church. Of greater significance than these movements is the Christian Endeavor Society, founded in 1881 in Portland, Maine, by the Rev. Francis E. Clark. So rapidly did this society grow that within a quarter of a century after its founding there were fifty thousand societies in several denominations. It soon became international in its scope and it has been an inspiration to thousands of young people in every part of the United States and the world. Nor do these organizations complete the list of undenominational movements within recent years. Numerous brotherhoods have been formed, undenominational in character, and such societies as the Woman's Christian Temperance Union, and the Anti-Saloon League, as well as the Y. M. and Y. W. C. A., depend on the cooperation of Christian people in all the churches to put over their programs.

Foreign missions and church unity.—In no field of Christian work is there a greater need for unity and cooperation than in foreign missions. It has been most unfortunate that denominational divisions have been transplanted to the mission fields—divisions that the native cannot possibly understand. At first there was no great harm done, as the field was so large, with little chance at overlapping; but since the number of missionaries has greatly increased, they have of necessity come into closer contact, and the danger of overlapping has thereby developed. To-day there are 350 foreign missionary boards, with more than 24,000 mission workers in the field. There are, for instance, 93 boards at work in China, 46 in Japan, 101 in India. In many large cities and populous centers, such as Tokyo and Foochow, numerous denominations are carrying on their work. This situation has led to the development of cooperative undertakings of various kinds on the mission fields. In China there are 20 educational institutions under interdenominational control, including 5 union universities. The Christian College for Women in Madras, India, is supported by a dozen missions. There are numerous interdenominational theological seminaries. Medical work is being conducted more and more through union hospitals and union medical schools. Another plan to prevent needless duplication on the mission field is the division of territory among the various denominations. One of the earliest examples of such division of territory was worked out in the Philippines on their transfer from Spain to the United States. All the Protestant churches planning to carry on work in the islands were called together, and there was formed the Evangelical Union of the Philippines, by which Baptists, Congregationalists, Methodists, Presbyterians, and United Brethren were assigned distinct fields. This plan of dividing missionary territory has made encouraging headway in North China, in Korea, and, more recently, in Mexico. The growing accord which is evident among the churches in the mission fields cannot but strengthen the ties of union among the churches in the homeland.

Progress of church federation.—The Evangelical Alliance, formed in London in 1846, may be considered the first step in church federation. This body was made up of fifty different evangelical bodies in Europe and America, and branches were soon established in nine European countries and in the United States. The great object of the alliance was to promote evangelical union with a view to increasing the effectiveness of Christian work, to promote the cause of religious freedom, and to further the cause of Christ everywhere. The branch alliance in the United States was formed in 1867, and through its influence many cooperative enterprises were undertaken. By the end of the last century the influence of the alliance was waning and in 1901 it gave way to a Federation of Churches and Christian Workers, which in turn was replaced in 1908 by the Federal Council of the Churches of Christ in America.

The Federal Council of the Churches of Christ in America.—The work of the Federal Council of the Churches has been summed up by its secretary as follows: "First of all, it is a clearing house for denominational and interdenominational activities; secondly, it speaks and acts in a representative capacity for the evangelical churches of America which constitute the council; thirdly, it acts for the churches in several departments of work through commissions and committees made up largely from the various boards and departments of its constituent bodies; and, fourthly, it develops local federations in cities and towns." Undoubtedly one of the great weaknesses of American Protestantism is its inability to speak with a united voice on matters of great moral and religious concern. The Federal Council is a step in the direction of uniting the thirty denominations that compose the council in such a way that they may be able to speak with a united voice on matters of general moral, social, and religious concern. The Federal Council proved its usefulness during the Great War, and in its work of mercy and relief since the war it has more than justified its existence.

The task of church unity.—There are two phases to the problem of church unity. The first is the task of achieving unity within each denomination; the second is the achieving of unity between different communions. It would seem that the former would be an easier task than the latter, but, as a matter of fact, neither is easy of accomplishment. The first obvious task, however, is to bring about unity within each denominational group. For instance, before there can be real unity between Methodists and Presbyterians, there must be real unity among Methodists and among Presbyterians. Certainly the first task to be performed by the Methodists is to heal the breach between the Methodist Episcopal Church and the Methodist Episcopal Church, South; and, just as certainly, the first task to be accomplished by the Presbyterians is the healing of the schism between the Presbyterian Church in the United States of America and the Presbyterian Church, South.

Progress toward denominational unity.—Considerable

progress has been made in recent years within several communions toward bringing about denominational unity. One of the best examples of such progress is the formation of the United Lutheran Church in 1918, composed of the General Synod, the General Council, and the United Synod of the South. The bodies uniting to form the United Lutheran Church surrendered their separate identities and consented to give up their names in the interest of union. Within the Presbyterian Church at large two unification movements have recently been consummated. In 1905 the Cumberland Presbyterian Church and the Presbyterian Church in the U. S. A. effected organic union, and in 1920 the Welsh Calvinistic Methodist Church was received into the Presbyterian Church in the U. S. A. Negotiations are now in progress for a closer union between the two great branches of the Presbyterians and also between the Presbyterian and the Reformed Churches. In the Methodist Episcopal Church negotiations have been in progress for several years toward healing the split created in 1844 by the controversy over slavery. Plans of union have been submitted to the last two General Conferences of both churches, and a joint commission representing both churches has perfected a plan which has at this writing been approval by the General Conference of the Methodist Episcopal Church.

Attitude of the various churches toward union with other churches.—The Congregationalists generally believe that "the churches will come and ought to come to some type of organic union." The Disciples favor the acceptance of "certain principles that they believe make for unity in the Church of Christ," such as a common name, a common creed, the Scriptures as sufficient for the rule of Christian life, a universal administration of the sacraments, and a common polity. The Lutheran Church favors church union based on a "definite statement of fundamental principles drawn from the Gospels and embodying the essential content of the Christian message." The Baptists favor a "combined impact of Christian forces upon the evil of the world," but since the Baptist Churches have no organic unity among themselves they therefore cannot have organic unity with other denominations. They believe that organic union with other churches is impossible. In 1920 the Presbyterian General Assembly approved a Plan of Union for Evangelical Churches in the United States and referred it to their presbyteries for their action. Within the Methodist Episcopal Church there is a large majority "ready for any feasible cooperation, friendly to definite federation, responsive to the appeal for organic union, and sympathetic with the ideals of those who seek to promote it, but incredulous as to its practicability." The Episcopalians have sought for years to obtain a working union with the Congregationalists especially, and some more or less definite plans have been formulated; but so far little has come of these efforts. The insistence on the part of the Episcopalians that episcopacy is essential to the being of the church is a hindrance to union with the nonepiscopal churches. While organic union of the Protestant churches in America is no doubt a long way off, the desire for such union is undoubtedly growing. As one Christian statesman puts it: "It needs no prophet to foretell that this movement is bound to increase in volume and momentum. Men may question, criticize, and resist it; but it can no more be held back than the tides of the sea."

QUESTIONS FOR DISCUSSION

1. What were the chief causes for divisions among Christian peoples during the colonial period? What were some of the factors working toward closer relations in the colonial period?

2. What have been the principal causes of division since independence?

3. What were some of the early interdenominational movements in the United States? Tell something of the organization and work of the American Bible Society.

4. In what ways have the Young Men's Christian Association and Young Women's Christian Association furthered the cause of church unity in the United States?

5. Describe some of the recent laymen's and young people's movements, and explain how these movements have furthered church union.

6. Why is there a particular need for church coopera-

tion in the various foreign missionary fields? What progress has been made in this respect?

7. What is the Federal Council of the Churches of Christ in America, and what purpose does this organization serve? Why is the inability of American Protestantism to speak with a united voice a great weakness? Is there any immediate chance of remedying this weakness?

8. Why is it necessary to achieve unity in each denominational group before interdenominational unity can take place? What progress has been made in recent years toward achieving denominational unity?

9. What is the attitude of the various Protestant churches toward organic union?

BIBLIOGRAPHY

For those who may desire to read further into the history of the churches in the United States the following books will be found useful:

The Foundations of American Nationality, by E. B. Greene (New York, 1922).

The Great Awakening in the Middle Colonies, by C. H. Maxson (Chicago, 1920).

The Great Revival in the West, 1797–1805, by C. C. Cleveland (Chicago, 1916).

The Rise of Methodism in the West, by W. W. Sweet (Nashville and Cincinnati, 1920).

The Frontier Spirit in American Christianity, by Peter G. Mode (New York, 1923).

The Schism in the Methodist Church, 1844, by J. N. Norwood (Alfred, New York, 1923).

The American Church History Series. This series contains thirteen volumes treating all the churches in the United States, as follows:

The Religious Forces in the United States, by H. K. Carroll.
Baptists, by A. H. Newman.
Congregationalists, by Williston Walker.
Lutherans, by H. E. Jacobs.
Methodists, by J. M. Buckley.
Presbyterians, by Robert Ellis Thompson.
Protestant Episcopal, by C. C. Tiffany.
The Reformed, Dutch; the Reformed, German and Moravian, by Corwin, Dubbs, and Hamilton.
Unitarians and Universalists, by Allen and Eddy.
Roman Catholics, by T. O'Gorman.
Methodist Episcopal, South; Presbyterians, South; United Presbyterians, and Cumberland Presbyterians, by Alexander, Johnson, Scouller, and Foster.

BIBLIOGRAPHY

Disciples, Friends, United Brethren, and Evangelical, by
Tyler, Thomas, Berger, and Spreng.
History of American Christianity, by L. W. Bacon.

The Larger Faith, by Charles R. Brown (Boston, 1923)
is an appreciation of the churches by one who knows them
as do few men in America.

The Year Book of the Churches (1923), published by
the Federal Council of the Churches of Christ in America,
is an especially valuable book for reference.

INDEX